THE ANCIENT ROMAN EMPIRE AND THE BRITISH EMPIRE IN INDIA

THE DIFFUSION OF ROMAN AND ENGLISH LAW THROUGHT THE WORLD

TWO HISTORICAL STUDIES

THE ANCIENT ROMAN EMPIRE AND THE BRITISH EMPIRE IN INDIA

THE DIFFUSION OF ROMAN AND ENGLISH LAW THROUGHT THE WORLD

TWO HISTORICAL STUDIES

BY

JAMES BRYCE

GYAN

Published by

GYAN

Gyan Publishing House
5, Ansari Road
Daryaganj, New Delhi-110002
Phone: 011-47034999, 9811692060
E-mail: books@gyanbooks.com

Distribution Network
gyanbooks.com
India, USA, Canada, UK, Australia

ISBN: 978-93-6433-796-0 (HB)
First Published, 1914

2nd Impression 2024

Printed at: Gyan Press, Delhi.

THE ANCIENT ROMAN EMPIRE AND THE BRITISH EMPIRE IN INDIA
THE DIFFUSION OF ROMAN AND ENGLISH LAW THROUGHT THE WORLD
AUTHOR: JAMES BRYCE

The Ancient Roman Empire and the British Empire in India

The Diffusion of Roman and English Law throughout the World

TWO HISTORICAL STUDIES

BY

JAMES BRYCE

Author of "The Holy Roman Empire," "The American Commonwealth," etc.

HUMPHREY MILFORD
OXFORD UNIVERSITY PRESS
LONDON, EDINBURGH, GLASGOW, NEW YORK
TORONTO, MELBOURNE, BOMBAY
1914

The Ancient Roman Empire and the British Empire in India

PREFACE

THESE two Essays appeared, along with a number of others bearing upon cognate historical and legal topics, in two volumes entitled *Studies in History and Jurisprudence* which I published some years ago. As it is now thought that they may have an interest for some readers, and especially for students of Indian history, who may not care to procure those volumes, they are now issued separately.

Both Essays have been revised throughout and brought up to date by the insertion of the figures of the latest census of India and by references to recent legislation. They do not, however, touch upon any questions of current Indian or English politics, for a discussion of these must needs involve matter of a controversial nature and might distract the reader's attention from those broad conclusions upon which historical students and impartial observers of India as it stands to-day are pretty generally agreed.

It is a pleasure to me to acknowledge and express my gratitude for the help which I have received in the work of revision from one of my oldest and most valued friends, Sir Courtenay Ilbert, G.C.B., formerly Legal Member of the Viceroy's Council in India and now Clerk of the House of Commons.

JAMES BRYCE.

August 11, 1913.

CONTENTS

Essay I

THE ROMAN EMPIRE AND THE BRITISH EMPIRE IN INDIA, 1-79

Essay II

THE EXTENSION OF ROMAN AND ENGLISH LAW THROUGHOUT THE WORLD, 80-133

I

THE ROMAN EMPIRE AND THE BRITISH EMPIRE IN INDIA

THERE is nothing in history more remarkable than the way in which two small nations created and learnt how to administer two vast dominions: the Romans their world-empire, into which all the streams of the political and social life of antiquity flowed and were blent; and the English their Indian Empire, to which are now committed the fortunes of more than three hundred millions of men. A comparison of these two great dominions in their points of resemblance and difference, points in which the phenomena of each serve to explain and illustrate the parallel phenomena of the other, is a subject which has engaged the attention of many philosophic minds, and is still far from being exhausted. Exhausted indeed it can scarcely be, for every year brings some changes in the conditions of Indian government, and nearly every year gives us some fresh light upon the organization and government of the Roman Empire. The observations and reflections contained in this Essay were suggested by a journey through India, which followed upon travels through most of the regions that once owned the sway of Rome; and I have tried to test them by conversations with many persons, both natives and Europeans, who know India thoroughly.

This Essay is intended to compare Rome and Britain as conquering and ruling powers, acquiring and administering dominions outside the original dwelling-place of their peoples, and impressing upon these dominions their own type of civilization. The following Essay compares the action of each as a power diffusing its law over the earth.

The comparison derives a special interest from a consideration of the position in which the world finds itself at the beginning of the twentieth century. The great civilized nations have spread themselves out so widely, and that with increasing rapidity during the last fifty years, as to have brought under their dominion or control nearly all the barbarous or semi-civilized races. Europe—that is to say the five or six races which we call the European branch of mankind—has annexed the rest of the earth, extinguishing some races, absorbing others, ruling others as subjects, and spreading over their native customs and beliefs a layer of European ideas which will sink deeper and deeper till the old native life dies out. Thus, while the face of the earth is being changed in a material sense by the application of European science, so it seems likely that within a measurable time European forms of thought and ways of life will come to prevail everywhere, except possibly in China, whose vast population may enable her to resist these solvent influences for several generations, and in some parts of the tropics where climate makes settlement by the white race difficult.

In this process whose agencies are migration, conquest, commerce, and finance, England has led the way and has achieved most. Russia, however, as well as France and Germany, have annexed vast areas inhabited by backward races. Even the United States has, by occupying the Hawaiian and the Philippine Islands, entered, somewhat to her own surprise, on the same path. Thus a new sort of unity is being created among mankind. This unity is seen in the bringing of every part of the globe into close relations, both commercial and political, with every other part. It is seen in the establishment of a few 'world languages' as vehicles of communication between many peoples, vehicles which carry to them the treasures of literature and science which the four or five leading nations have gathered. It is seen in the diffusion of a civilization which is everywhere the same in its material aspects, and is tolerably uniform even on its intellectual side, since it teaches men to think on similar lines and to apply similar methods of scientific inquiry. The process has been going on for some centuries. In our own day it advances so swiftly that we can almost foresee the time when it will be complete. It is one of the great events in the history of the world.

Yet it is not altogether a new thing. A similar process went on in the ancient world from the time of Alexander the Macedonian to that of Alaric the Visigoth. The Greek type of civilization, and to some extent the Greek population also, spread out over the regions around the eastern Mediterranean and the Euxine. Presently the conquests of Rome brought all these regions, as well as the western countries as far as Caledonia, under one government. This produced a uniform type of civilization which was Greek on the side of thought, of literature, and of art, Roman on the side of law and institutions. Then came Christianity which, in giving to all these countries one religion and one standard of morality, created a still deeper sense of unity among them. Thus the ancient world, omitting the barbarous North and the semi-civilized heathen who dwelt beyond the Euphrates, became unified, the backward races having been raised, at least in the upper strata of their population, to the level of the more advanced. One government, one faith, and two languages, were making out of the mass of races and kingdoms that had existed before the Macedonian conquest, a single people who were at once a Nation and a World Nation.

The process was not quite complete when it was interrupted by the political dissolution of the Roman dominion, first through the immigrations of the Teutonic peoples from the north, and afterwards by the terrible strokes which Arab conquerors from the south-east dealt at the already weakened empire. The results that had been attained were not wholly lost, for Europe clung to the Græco-Romano-Christian civilization, though in a lowered form and with a diminished sense of intellectual as well as of political unity. But that civilization was not able to extend itself further, save by slow degrees over the north and towards the north-east. Several centuries passed. Then, at first faintly from the twelfth century onwards, afterwards more swiftly from the middle of the fifteenth century, when the intellectual impulse given by the Renaissance began to be followed by the rapid march of geographical discovery along the coasts of Africa, in America, and in the further east, the process was resumed. We have watched its later stages with our own eyes. It embraces a far vaster field than did the earlier one, the field of the whole earth. As we watch it, we are naturally led to ask what light the earlier effort of Nature to gather men together under one type of civilization throws on this later one. As Rome was the principal agent in the earlier, so has England been in the later effort. England has sent her language, her commerce, her laws and institutions forth from herself over an even wider and more populous area than that whose races were moulded into new forms by the laws and institutions of Rome. The conditions are, as we shall see, in many respects different. Yet there is in the parallel enough to make it instructive for the present, and possibly significant for the future.

The dominions of England beyond the seas are, however, not merely too locally remote from one another, but also too diverse in their character to be compared as one whole with the dominions of Rome, which were contiguous in space, and were all governed on the same system. The Britannic Empire falls into three territorial groups,—the Dominions (as the self-governing colonies are now called), the Crown colonies, and the Indian territories ruled by or dependent on the sovereign of Britain. Of these three groups, since they cannot be treated together, being ruled on altogether different principles, it is one group only that can usefully be selected for comparison with the Roman Empire. India contains that one group. She is fitter for our purpose than either of the other two groups because the Dominions are not subject territories administered from England, but new Englands planted far away beyond the oceans, reproducing, each in its own way, the features of the constitution and government of the old country, while the Crown colonies are so scattered and so widely diverse in the character of their inhabitants that they cannot profitably be dealt with as one body. Jamaica, Cyprus, Basutoland, Singapore, and Gibraltar, have little in common except their dependence on Downing Street. Neither set of colonies is sufficiently like the dominion of Rome to make it possible for us to draw parallels between them and it. India, however, is a single subject territory, and India is compact, governed on the same principles and by the same methods over an area not indeed as wide as that of the Roman Empire but more populous than the Roman Empire was in its palmiest days. British India (including Burma) covers about 1,087,204 square miles, and the Protected States (including Kashmir, but not Nepal and Bhotan), 673,393 square miles, making a total of 1,760,597 square miles, with a population of 315 millions[1]. The area of the territories included in the Roman Empire

[1] These figures were the latest available in 1912. The exact population of British India was then given as 315,132,537 of whom 244,267,542 were in British India, 70,864,995 in Protected States.

at its greatest extent (when Dacia and the southern part of what was then Caledonia and is now Scotland belonged to it) may have been nearly 2,500,000 square miles. The population of that area is now, upon a very rough estimate, about 210 millions. What it was in ancient times we have no data even for guessing, but it must evidently have been much smaller, possibly not 100 millions, for although large regions, such as parts of Asia Minor and Tunisia, now almost deserted, were then filled by a dense industrial population, the increase in the inhabitants of France and England, for instance, has far more than compensated this decline.

The Spanish Empire in America as it stood in the sixteenth and seventeenth centuries was still vaster in area, as is the Russian Empire in Asia to-day [2]. But the population of Spanish America was extremely small in comparison with that of the Roman Empire or that of India, and its organization much looser and less elaborate. There was never one colonial government for all the Spanish American dominions; each Viceroyalty and Captaincy General (in later days) was in direct and separate relations with the Council of the Indies in Spain. Both the Spanish and the Russian Empires, however, furnish illustrations which we shall have occasion presently to note.

Of all the dominions which the ancient world saw, it is only that of Rome that can well be compared with any modern civilized State. The monarchies of the Assyrian and Egyptian conquerors, like those of the Seleucid kings and of the Sassanid dynasty in Persia, stood on a far lower level of culture and administrative efficiency than did the Roman. Neither was there in the Middle Ages any far stretching dominion fit to be matched with that of Rome, for the great Ommiad

[2] The total area of the Russian Empire exceeds 8,000,000 square miles, and the population is about 130,000,000.

Khalifate and the Mogul monarchy in India were both of them mere aggregates of territories, not really unified by any administrative system, while the authority or suzerainty of the Chinese sovereigns over Turkistan, Mongolia, and Tibet presents even fewer points of resemblance. So when we wish to examine the methods and the results of British rule in India by the light of any other dominion exercised under conditions even remotely similar, it is to the Roman Empire of the centuries between Augustus and Honorius that we must go.

When one speaks of conditions even remotely similar one must frankly admit the existence of an obvious and salient point of contrast. Rome stood in the middle of her dominions, Britain stands, by the Red Sea route, six thousand miles from the nearest part of hers. She can reach them only by water, and she conquered them by troops which had been sent around the Cape over some thirteen thousand miles of ocean. Here there is indeed an unlikeness of the utmost significance. Yet, without minimizing the importance of the contrast, we must remember that Britain can in our own day communicate more quickly with the most distant part of her territories than Rome could with hers. It takes only twenty days to reach any part of British India (except Kashmir and Upper Assam) from London. But it took a nimble, or as Herodotus says, a 'well girt traveller,' perhaps forty days from Rome to reach Derr on the Nile, the last fortress in Nubia where Roman masonry can be seen, or Gori, at the south foot of the Caucasus, also a Roman stronghold, or Old Kilpatrick (near Dumbarton) where the rampart of the Emperor Antoninus Pius touches the Clyde; not to add that the sea part of these journeys might be much longer if the winds were adverse. News could be carried not much faster than an official could travel, whereas Britain is, by the electric telegraph, in hourly communication with every part of India: and the difference in speed between the movement of an army and that of a traveller was, of course, greater in ancient times than it is now.

Thus, for the purposes both of war and of administration, England is better placed than was Rome as respects those outlying parts of the Roman Empire which were most exposed to attack. Dangers are more quickly known at head quarters; troops can reach the threatened frontier in a shorter time; errors in policy can be more adequately corrected, because explanations can be asked, and blundering officials can be more promptly dismissed. Nevertheless the remoteness of India has had results of the highest moment in making her relation to England far less close than was that of Rome to the provinces.

This point will be considered presently. Meantime our comparison may begin with the points in which the two Empires resemble and illustrate one another. The first of these turns upon the circumstances of their respective origins.

Empire is retained, says a famous maxim, by the same arts whereby it was won. Some Empires have been won easily. Spain acquired hers through the pertinacity and daring of a Genoese sailor, followed by expeditions of such adventurers as Cortes and Pizarro, who went forth to conquer on their own initiative, although in the name and for the benefit of their sovereign. She had comparatively little fighting to do, for the only opponents she encountered who added to valour some slight tincture of civilization were the Aztecs and their allies in Mexico. Among the wilder tribes one alone opposed a successful resistance, the Araucanians of Chile.

Russia has met with practically no opposition in occupying her vast territories in Northern Asia all the way to the Pacific; though further south she had some sharp tussles with the nomad Turkmans, and tedious conflicts both with Shamyl and with the Circassians in the Caucasus. But both Rome and England had to fight long and fight hard for what they won. The progress of Roman and British expansion illustrates the remark of Oliver Cromwell that no one goes so far as he who does not know whither he is going. Neither power set out with a purpose of conquest, such as Alexander the Great, and perhaps Cyrus, had planned and carried out before them. Even as Polybius, writing just after the destruction of Carthage in B. C. 146, already perceived that Rome was, by the strength of her government and the character of her people, destined to be the dominant power of the civilized world, so it was prophesied immediately after the first victories of Clive that the English would come to be the masters of all India. Each nation was drawn on by finding that one conquest led almost inevitably to another because restless border tribes had to be subdued, because formidable neighbours seemed to endanger the safety of subjugated but often discontented provinces, because allies inferior in strength passed gradually into the position first of dependents and then of subjects.

The Romans however, though they did not start out with the notion of conquering even Italy, much less the Mediterranean world, came to enjoy fighting for its own sake, and were content with slight pretexts for it. For several centuries they were always more or less at war somewhere. The English went to India as traders, with no intention of fighting anybody, and were led into the acquisition of territory partly in order to recoup themselves for the expensive efforts they had made to support their first allies, partly that they might get revenue for the East India Company's shareholders, partly in order to counterwork the schemes of the French, who were at once their enemies in Europe and their rivals in the East. One may find a not too fanciful analogy to the policy of the English in the days of Clive, when they were drawn further and further into Indian conflicts by their efforts to check the enterprises of Dupleix and Lally, in the policy of the Romans when they entered Sicily to prevent Carthage from establishing her control over it. In both cases an effort which was advocated as self-protective led to a long series of wars and annexations.

Rome did not march so swiftly from conquest to conquest as did England. Not to speak of the two centuries during which she was making herself supreme in Italy, she began to conquer outside its limits from the opening of the First Punic War in B. C. 264, and did not acquire Egypt till B. C. 30, and South Britain till A. D. 43-85 [1]. Her Eastern conquests were all the easier because Alexander the Great's victories, and the wars waged by his successors, had broken up and denationalized the East, much as the Mogul conquerors afterwards paved the way for the English in India. England's first territorial gains were won at Plassy in A. D. 1757 [2]: her latest acquisition was the occupation of Mandalay in 1885. Her work was done in a century and a quarter, while that of Rome took fully three centuries. But England had two great advantages. Her antagonists were immeasurably inferior to her in arms as well as in discipline. As early as A. D. 1672 the great Leibnitz had in a letter to Lewis XIV pointed out the weakness of the Mogul Empire; and about the same time Bernier, a French physician resident at the Court of Aurungzeb, declared that 20,000 French troops under Condé or Turenne could conquer all India [3]. A small European force, and even a small native force drilled and led by Europeans, was as capable of routing huge Asiatic armies as the army of Alexander had proved capable

[1] Dacia was taken by Trajan in A. D. 107, and lost in A. D. 251. Mesopotamia and Arabia Petraea were annexed by Trajan about the same time, but the former was renounced so soon afterwards that its conquest can hardly be considered a part of the regular process of expansion.

[2] Territorial authority may be said to date from the grant of the Diwani in 1765.

[3] See the admirably clear and thoughtful book of Sir A. C. Lyall, *Rise of British Dominion in India*, pp. 52 and 126.

of overthrowing the immensely more numerous hosts of Darius Codomannus. Moreover, the moment when the English appeared on the scene was opportune. The splendid Empire of Akbar was crumbling to pieces. The Mahratta confederacy had attained great military power, but at the battle of Paniput, in 1761, it received from the Afghans under Ahmed Shah Durani a terrific blow which for the time arrested its conquests. Furthermore, India, as a whole, was divided into numerous principalities, the feeblest of which lay on the coasts of the Bay of Bengal. These principalities were frequently at war with one another, and glad to obtain European aid in their strife.

And England had a third advantage in the fact that she encountered the weakest of her antagonists first. Had she, in those early days when her forces were slender, been opposed by the valour of Marathas or Sikhs, instead of the feeble Bengalis and Madrassis, her ambitions might have been nipped in the bud. When she found herself confronted by those formidable foes she had already gained experience and had formed a strong native army. But when the Romans strove against the Achaean League and Macedon they had to fight troops all but equal to themselves. When Carthage was their antagonist, they found in Hamilcar a commander equal, and in Hannibal a commander superior to any one they could send against him. These earlier struggles so trained Rome to victory that her later conquests were made more easily. The triumphs of the century before and the century after Julius Caesar were won either over Asiatics, who had discipline but seldom valour, or over Gauls, Iberians, Germans, and Caledonians, who had valour but not discipline. Occasional reverses were due to the imprudence of a general, or to an extreme disparity of forces; for the Romans, like the English, did not hesitate to meet greatly superior numbers. The defeat of Crassus by the Parthians and the catastrophe which befell Varus in the forests of Paderborn find a parallel in the disastrous retreat of the English army from Cabul in 1843. Except on such rare occasions, the supremacy of Roman arms was never seriously challenged, nor was any great calamity suffered till the barbarian irruption into Italy in the reign of Marcus Aurelius. A still graver omen for the future was the overthrow of Valerian by the Persians in A. D. 260. The Persians were inferior in the arts of civilization and probably in discipline: but the composition of the Roman armies was no longer what it had been three centuries earlier, for the peasantry of Italy, which had formed the kernel of their strength, were no longer available. As the provincial subjects became less and less warlike, men from beyond the frontier were enrolled, latterly in bodies under their native chiefs —Germans, or Arabs, or, in still later days, Huns,—just as the native army in British India, nearly all of which has now become far more peaceful than it was a century ago, is recruited by Pathans and Ghurkas from the hills outside British territory as well as by the most warlike among the Indian subjects of the Crown. The danger of the practice is obvious. Rome was driven to it for want of Roman fighting-men [1]. England guards against its risks by having a considerable force of British troops alongside her native army.

The fact that their dominions were acquired by force of arms exerted an enduring effect upon the Roman Empire and continues to exert it upon the British in imprinting upon their rule in India a permanently military character. The Roman administration began with this character, and never lost it, at least in the frontier provinces. The governors were proconsuls or propraetors, or other officials, intrusted with the exercise of an authority in its origin military rather than civil.

[1] And indeed the employment of these enlisted barbarians to resist the outer barbarians probably prolonged the life of the Empire.

A governor's first duty was to command the troops stationed in the province. The camps grew into towns, and that which had been a group of *canabae* or market stalls, a sort of bazaar for the service of the camp, sometimes became a municipality. One of the most efficient means of unifying the Empire was found in the bringing of soldiers born in one part of it to be quartered for many years together in another. Military distinction was open to every subject, and military distinction might lead to the imperial throne. So the English in India are primarily soldiers. True it is that they went to India three centuries ago as traders, that it was out of a trading company that their power arose, and that this trading company did not disappear till 1858. The covenanted civil service, to which Clive for instance belonged, began as a body of commercial clerks. Nothing sounds more pacific. But the men of the sword very soon began to eclipse the men of the quill and account book. Being in the majority, they do so still, although for forty years there have been none but petty frontier wars. Society is not in India, as it is in England, an ordinary civil society occupied with the works and arts of peace, with an extremely small military element. It is military society, military first and foremost, though with an infusion of civilian officials, and in some towns with a small infusion of lawyers and merchants, as well as a still smaller infusion of missionaries. Military questions occupy every one's thoughts and talk. A great deal of administrative or diplomatic work is done, and often extremely well done, by officers in civil employment. Many of the railways are primarily strategic lines, as were the Roman roads. The railway stations are often placed, for military reasons, at a distance from the towns they serve: and the cantonments where the Europeans, civilians as well as soldiers, reside, usually built some way off from the native cities, have themselves, as happened in the Roman Empire, grown into regular towns. The traveller from peaceful England feels himself, except perhaps in Bombay, surrounded by an atmosphere of gunpowder all the time he stays in India.

Before we pass from the military aspects of the comparison let it be noted that both Empires have been favoured in their extension and their maintenance by the frontiers which Nature had provided. The Romans, when once they had conquered Numidia, Spain, and Gaul, had the ocean and nothing but the ocean (save for the insignificant exception of barbarous Mauretania) to the west and north-west of them, an awesome and untravelled ocean, from whose unknown further shore no enemy could appear. To the south they were defended by the equally impassable barrier of a torrid and waterless desert, stretching from the Nile to the Atlantic. It was only on the north and east that there were frontiers to be defended; and these two sides remained the quarters of danger, because no natural barrier, arresting the progress of armies or constituting a defensible frontier, could be found without pushing all the way to the Baltic in one direction or to the ranges of Southern Kurdistan, perhaps even to the deserts of Eastern Persia in the other. The north and the east ultimately destroyed Rome. The north sent in those Teutonic tribes which occupied the western provinces and at last Italy herself, and those Slavonic tribes which settled between the Danube, the Aegean, and the Adriatic, and permeated the older population of the Hellenic lands. Perhaps the Emperors would have done better for the Empire (whatever might have been the ultimate loss to mankind) if, instead of allowing themselves to be disheartened by the defeat of Varus, they had pushed their conquests all the way to the Baltic and the Vistula, and turned the peoples of North and Middle Germany into provincial Romans. The undertaking would not have been beyond the resources of the Empire in its vigorous prime, and would have been remunerative, if not in money, at any rate in the way of providing a supply of fighting-men for the army. So too the Emperors might possibly have saved much suffering to their Romanized subjects in South Britain had they followed up the expedition of Agricola and subdued the peoples of Caledonia and Ierne, who afterwards became disagreeable as Picts and Scots. The east was the home of the Parthians, of the Persians, so formidable to the Byzantine Emperors in the days of Kobad and Chosroes Anushirwan, and of the tribes which in the seventh and eighth centuries, fired by the enthusiasm of a new faith and by the prospect of booty, overthrew the Roman armies and turned Egypt, Syria, Africa, Spain, and ultimately the greater part of Asia Minor into Muhamadan kingdoms. Had Rome been menaced on the south and west as she was generally menaced on the east and sometimes on the north, her Empire could hardly have lived so long. Had she possessed a natural barrier on the east like that which the Sahara provided on the south she might have found it easy to resist, and not so very hard even to subjugate, the fighting races of the north.

Far more fortunate has been the position of the English in India. No other of the great countries of the world is protected by such a stupendous line of natural entrenchments as India possesses in the chain of the Himalayas from Attock and Peshawur in the west to the point where, in the far east, the Tsanpo emerges from Tibet to become in Upper Assam the Brahmaputra. Not only is this mountain mass the loftiest and most impassable to be found anywhere on our earth; it is backed by a wide stretch of high and barren country, so thinly peopled as to be incapable of constituting a menace to those who live in the plains south of the Himalayas. And in point of fact the relations, commercial as well as political, of India with Tibet, and with the Chinese who are in a somewhat shadowy way suzerains of Tibet[1], have been, at least in historical times, extremely scanty.

On the east, India is divided from the Indo-Chinese peoples, Talains, Burmese and Shans, by a belt of almost impenetrable hill and forest country: nor have these peoples ever been formidable neighbours. It is only at its north-western angle, between Peshawur and Quetta (for south of Quetta as far as the Arabian Sea there are deserts behind the mountains and the Indus) that India is vulnerable. The rest of the country is protected by a wide ocean. Accordingly the masters of India have had only two sets of foes to fear—European maritime powers who may arrive by sea after a voyage which, until our own time, was a voyage of three or four months, and land powers who, coming from the side of Turkistan or Persia, may find their way, as did Alexander the Great and Nadir Shah, through difficult passes into the plains of the Punjab and Sindh. This singular natural isolation of India, as it facilitated the English conquest by preventing the native princes from forming alliances with or obtaining help from powers beyond the mountains or the sea, so has it also enabled the English to maintain their hold with an army extraordinarily small in proportion to the population of the country. The total strength of the Roman military establishment in the days of Trajan, was for an area of some two and a half millions of square miles and a population of possibly one hundred millions, between 280,000 and 320,000 men. Probably four-fifths of this force was stationed on the Rhine, the Danube, and the Euphrates. There were so few in most of the inner

[1] In 1904 an expedition officially described as "a mission accompanied by a military escort" was sent to Tibet to endeavour to adjust some outstanding difficulties. Its approach was unsuccessfully resisted by a Tibetan force at Gyantse; Lhassa was reached and a treaty signed there September 7, 1904, and most of the troops had returned to India by November. In 1906 China signified her adhesion to the settlement effected under this treaty, but the precise nature of her relations to Tibet still remains in doubt as between her and the Government of India which refuses to admit what she tries to claim.

provinces that, as some one said, the nations wondered where were the troops that kept them in subjection.

The peace or 'established' strength of the British army in India is 237,000 men, of whom 159,000 are natives and 78,000 Englishmen. To these there may be added the so-called 'active reserve' of natives who have served with the colours, about 34,000 men, and about 30,000 European volunteers. Besides these there are of course the troops of the native princes, estimated at about 100,000 men, many of them, however, far from effective. But as these troops, though a source of strength while their masters are loyal, might under altered circumstances be conceivably a source of danger, they can hardly be reckoned as part of the total force disposable by the British Government. Recently, however, about 18,000 of them have been organized as special contingents of the British army, inspected and advised by British officers, and fit to take their place with regiments of the line [1].

It would obviously be impossible to defend such widely extended dominions by a force of only 237,000 or 267,000 men, but for the remoteness of all possibly dangerous assailants. The only strong land neighbour is Russia, the nearest point of whose territories in the Pamirs is a good long way from the present British outposts, with a very lofty and difficult country behind. The next nearest is France on the Mekong River, some 200 miles from British Burma, though a shorter distance from Native States under British influence. As for sea powers, not only is Europe a long way off, but the navy of Britain holds the sea. It was by her command of the sea that Britain won India. Were she to cease to hold it, her position there would be insecure indeed.

In another respect also the sharp severance of India from all the surrounding countries may be deemed to have proved a benefit to the English. It has relieved

[1] An account of this new Imperial Service force may be found in the *Imperial Gazetteer* of India, Vol. IV, p. 87 (edn. of 1907).

them largely if not altogether from the temptation to go on perpetually extending their borders by annexing contiguous territory. When they had reached the natural boundaries of the Himalayas and the ranges of Afghanistan, they stopped. Beyond these lie rugged and unprofitable highlands, and still more unprofitable wildernesses. In two regions only was an advance possible: and in those two regions they have yielded to temptation. They have crossed the southern part of the Soliman mountains into Baluchistan in search for a more 'scientific' frontier, halting for the present on the Amram range, north-west of Quetta, where from the Khojak heights the eye, ranging over a dark-brown arid plain, descries seventy miles away the cliff that hangs over the city of Kandahar. Whether their interests in Southern Persia will ever lead them still further west beyond the deserts of Seistan remains doubtful. They moved on from Arakhan and Tenasserim into Lower Burma, whence in 1885 they conquered Upper Burma and proclaimed their suzerainty over some of the Shan principalities lying further to the east, and advanced their outposts to the frontier of China. But for the presence of France in these regions, which makes them desire to keep Siam in existence as a so-called 'Buffer State,' "manifest destiny" might probably lead them ultimately eastward across the rivers Menam and Mekong to Annam and Cochin China [1].

The Romans too sought for a scientific frontier, and hesitated often as to the line they should select, sometimes pushing boldly eastward beyond the Rhine and the Euphrates, sometimes receding to those rivers. Not till the time of Hadrian did they create a regular system of frontier defence, strengthened at many points by fortifications, among which the forts that lie along the

[1] In 1904 an arrangement was made between the British and French Governments by which it was agreed that the influence of the former should not be opposed by the latter in the country west of the basin of the Menam.

Roman Wall from the Tyne to the Solway are perhaps the best preserved. A remarkable one may be seen in Western Germany on the heights of the Taunus not far from Nauheim. So the English wavered for a time between the line of the Indus and that of the Soliman range; so in the wild mountain region beyond Kashmir they have, within the last few years, alternately occupied and retired from the remote outpost of Chitral. It has been their good fortune to have been obliged to fortify a comparatively small number of points, and all of these are on the north-west frontier.

There have been those who would urge them to occupy Afghanistan and entrench themselves therein to resist a possible Russian invasion. But for the present wiser counsels have prevailed. Afghanistan is a more effective barrier in the hands of its own fierce tribes than it would be as a part of British territory. A parallel may be drawn between the part it has played of late years and that which Armenia played in the ancient world from the days of Augustus to those of Heraclius. Both countries had been the seats of short-lived Empires, Armenia in the days of Tigranes, Afghanistan in those of Ahmed Shah. Both are wild and rugged regions, the dwelling-places of warlike races. Christian Armenia was hostile from religious sentiment to the heathen enemies whom Rome had in the fifth and sixth centuries to fear, the Persian Fire-worshippers. Musulman Afghanistan dreads the power of Christian Russia. But the loyalty or friendship of the Armenian princes was not always proof against the threats of the formidable Sassanids, and the action of the Afghans has been an element of uncertainty and anxiety to the British rulers of India [1].

[1] By a convention signed in August, 1907, it was agreed between the British and Russian Governments that Afghanistan should be thereafter deemed outside the Russian sphere of influence and that all the political relations of Russia with the Afghans should be conducted through Great Britain, the latter therewith declaring her intention not to change the political status of Afghanistan and to exercise only a pacific influence there.

To make forces so small as those on which Rome relied and those which now defend British India adequate for the work they have to do, good means of communication are indispensable. It was one of the first tasks of the Romans to establish such means. They were the great—indeed one may say, the only—road builders of antiquity. They began this policy before they had completed the conquest of Italy; and it was one of the devices which assured their supremacy throughout that peninsula. They followed it out in Gaul, Spain, Africa, Britain, and the East, doing their work so thoroughly that in Britain some of the Roman roads continued to be the chief avenues of travel down till the eighteenth century. So the English have been in India a great engineering people, constructing lines of communication, first roads and afterwards railways, on a scale of expenditure unknown to earlier ages. The potentates of elder days, Hindu rajahs, and subsequently Pathans and Moguls, with other less famous Musulman dynasties, have left their memorials in temples and mosques, in palaces and tombs. The English are commemorating their sway by railway works, by tunnels and cuttings, by embankments and bridges. If India were to relapse into barbarism the bridges, being mostly of iron, would after a while perish, and the embankments would in time be swept away by tortential rains, but the rock-cuttings and the tunnels would remain, as the indestructible paving-stones of the Roman roads, and such majestic bridges as the Pont du Gard near Nismes, remain to witness to the skill and thoroughness with which a great race did its work.

The opening up of India by railroads suggests not a few interesting questions which, however, I can do no more than indicate here. Railroad construction has imposed upon the Indian exchequer a strain all the heavier because some lines, especially those on the north-west frontier, having been undertaken from strategic rather than commercial motives, will yield no revenue at all proportionate to their cost. It has been suggested that although railroads were meant to benefit the peasantry, they may possibly have increased the risk of famine, since they induce the producer to export the grain which was formerly locally stored up in good years to meet the scarcity of bad years. The comparative quickness with which food can be carried by rail into a famine area does not—so it is argued—compensate for the loss of these domestic reserves. Railways, bringing the numerous races that inhabit India into a closer touch with one another than was possible before, are breaking down, slowly but surely, the demarcations of caste, and are tending towards an assimilation of the jarring elements, racial and linguistic, as well as religious, which have divided India into a number of distinct, and in many cases hostile, groups. Centuries may elapse before this assimilation can become a source of political danger to the rulers of the country: yet we discern the faint beginnings of the process now, especially in the more educated class. The Roman roads, being highways of commerce as well as of war, contributed powerfully to draw together the peoples whom Rome ruled into one imperial nationality. But this was a process which, as we shall presently note, was for Rome an unmixed gain, since it strengthened the cohesion of an Empire whose inhabitants had every motive for loyalty to the imperial Government, if not always to the particular sovereign. The best efforts of Britain may not succeed in obtaining a similar attachment from her Indian subjects, and their union into a body animated by one national sentiment might become an element of danger against which she has never yet been required to take precautions.

The excellence of the highways of communication provided by the wise energy of the Romans and of the English has contributed not only to the easier defence of the frontiers of both Empires, but also to the maintenance of a wonderfully high standard of internal peace and order. Let any one think of the general state of the ancient world before the conquests of Rome, and let him then think of the condition not merely of India after the death of the Emperor Aurungzeb, but of the chief European countries as they stood in the seventeenth century, if he wishes to appreciate what Rome did for her subjects, or what England has done in India. In some parts of Europe private war still went on two hundred and fifty years ago. Almost everywhere robber bands made travelling dangerous and levied tribute upon the peasantry. Even in the eighteenth century, and even within our own islands, Rob Roy MacGregor raided the farmers of Lennox, and landlords in Connaught fought pitched battles with one another at the head of their retainers. Even a century ago the coasts of the Mediterranean were ravaged by Barbary pirates, and brigandage reigned unchecked through large districts of Italy. But in the best days of the Roman Empire piracy was unknown; the peasantry were exempt from all exactions except those of the tax-gatherer; and the great roads were practically safe for travellers. Southern and western Europe, taken as a whole, would seem to have enjoyed better order under Hadrian and the Antonines than was enjoyed again until nearly our own times. This was the more remarkable because the existence of slavery must have let loose upon society, in the form of runaway slaves, a good many dangerous characters. Moreover, there remained some mountainous regions where the tribes had been left practically to themselves under their own rude customs. These enclaves of barbarism within civilized territory, such as was Albania, in the central mountain knot of which no traces of Roman building have been found, and the Isaurian country in Asia Minor, and possibly the Cantabrian land on the borders of south-western Gaul and northern Spain, where the Basque tongue still survives, do not appear to have seriously interfered with the peace and well-being of the settled population which dwelt around them, probably because the mountaineers knew that it was only by good behaviour that they could obtain permission to enjoy the measure of independence that had been left to them. The parts of provincial Africa which lay near the desert were less orderly, because it was not easy to get behind the wild tribes who had the Sahara at their back.

The internal peace of the Roman Empire was, however, less perfect than that which has been established within the last sixty years in India. Nothing surprises the visitor from Europe so much as the absolute confidence with which he finds himself travelling alone and unguarded across this vast country, through mountains and jungles, among half savage tribes whose languages he does not know, and that without seeing, save at rare intervals, any sign of European administration. Nor is this confined to British India. It is almost the same in Native States. Even along the lofty forest and mountain frontier that separates the native (protected) principality of Sikkim from Nepal—the only really independent Indian State—an Englishman may journey without weapons and alone, except for a couple of native attendants, for a week or more. When he asks his friends at Darjiling, before he starts, whether he ought to take a revolver with him, they smile at the question. For native travellers, especially in Native States, there is not so complete a security inasmuch as here and there bands of brigands called dacoits infest the tracks, and rob, sometimes the wayfarer, sometimes the peasant, escaping into the recesses of the jungle when the police are after them. But dacoity, though it occasionally breaks out afresh in a few districts, has become much less frequent than formerly. The practice of Thuggi, which seventy years ago still caused many murders, has been extirpated by the unceasing energy of British officers. Crimes of violence show a percentage to the population which appears small when one considers how many wild tribes remain. The native of course suffers from violence more frequently than does the European, whose prestige of race, backed by the belief that punishment will surely follow on any injury done to him, keeps him safe in the wildest districts [1].

I have referred to the enclaves within the area of the Roman Empire where rude peoples were allowed to live after their own fashion so long as they did not disturb the peace of their more civilized neighbours. One finds the Indian parallel to these districts, not so much in the Native States, for these are often as advanced in the arts of life, and, in a very few instances, almost as well administered, as British territory, but rather in the hill tribes, which in parts of central, of north-western, and of southern India, have retained their savage or semi-savage customs, under their own chiefs, within the provinces directly subject to the Crown. These tribes, as did, and still do, the Albanians and Basques, cleave to their primitive languages, and cleave also to their primitive forms of ghost-worship or nature-worship, though Hinduism is beginning to lay upon them its tenacious grasp. Of one another's lives and property they are not very careful. But they are awed by the European and leave him unmolested.

The success of the British, like that of the Roman administration in securing peace and good order, has been due, not merely to a sense of the interest every government has in maintaining conditions which, because favourable to industry are favourable also to rev-

[1] An incident like the murder in 1891 of the Chief Commissioner of Assam at Manipur, a small Protected State in the hill country between Assam and Burma, is so rare and excites so much surprise and horror as to be the best proof of the general tranquillity. In that case there had been some provocation, though not on the part of the Chief Commissioner himself, an excellent man of conciliatory temper.

enue, but also to the high ideal of the duties of a ruler which both nations have set before themselves. Earlier Empires, like those of the Persian Achaemenids or of the successors of Alexander, had been content to tax their subjects and raise armies from them. No monarch, except perhaps some of the Ptolemies in Egypt, seems to have set himself to establish a system from which his subjects would benefit. Rome, with larger and higher views, gave to those whom she conquered some compensations in better administration for the national independence she extinguished. Her ideals rose as she acquired experience, and as she came to feel the magnificence of her position. Even under the Republic attempts were made to check abuses of power on the part of provincial governors. The proceedings against Verres, which we know so well because Cicero's speeches against that miscreant have been preserved, are an instance of steps taken in the interests of a province whose discontent was so little likely to harm Rome that no urgent political necessity prescribed them. Those proceedings showed how defective was the machinery for controlling or punishing a provincial governor; and it is clear enough that a great deal of extortion and misfeasance went on under proconsuls and propraetors in the later days of the Republic, to the enrichment, not only of those functionaries, but of the hungry swarm who followed them, including bright young men from Rome, who, like the poet Catullus, were made for better things [1]. With the establishment of a monarchy administration improved. The Emperor had a more definite responsibility for securing the welfare and contentment of the provinces than had been felt by the Senate or by the jurors who composed the courts of the Republic, swayed as they were by party interest or passion, not

[1] Poems x and xxviii. It is some comfort to know that Catullus obtained in Bithynia only themes for some of his most charming verses (see poems iv and xlvi). Gains would probably have been ill-gotten.

to speak of more sordid motives. He was, moreover, able to give effect to his wishes more promptly and more effectively. He could try an incriminated official in the way he thought best, and mete out appropriate punishment. It may indeed be said that the best proof of the incompetence of the Republican system for the task of governing the world, and of the need for the concentration of powers in a single hand, is to be found in the scandals of provincial administration, scandals which, so far as we can judge, could not have been remedied without a complete change either in the tone and temper of the ruling class at Rome, or in the ancient constitution itself.

On this point the parallel with the English in India is interesting, dissimilar as the circumstances were. The English administration began with extortions and corruptions. Officials were often rapacious, sometimes unjust, in their dealings with the native princes. But the statesmen and the public opinion of England, even in the latter half of the eighteenth century, had higher standards than those of Rome in the days of Sulla and Cicero, while the machinery which the House of Commons provided for dealing with powerful offenders was more effective than the Roman method of judicial proceedings before tribunals which could be, and frequently were, bribed. The first outbreak of greed and corruption in Bengal was dealt with by the strong hand of Clive in 1765. It made so great an impression at home as to give rise to a provision in a statute of 1773, making offences against the provisions of that Act or against the natives of India, punishable by the Court of King's Bench in England. By Pitt's Act of 1784, a Special Court, consisting of three judges, four peers, and six members of the House of Commons, was created for the trial in England of offences committed in India. This singular tribunal, which has been compared with the *quaestio perpetua* (*de pecuniis repetundis*) of Senators created by a Roman statute of B. C. 149 to try offences committed by Roman officials against provincials, has never acted, or even been summoned [1]. Soon after it came the famous trial which is more familiar to Englishmen than any other event in the earlier relations of England and India. The impeachment of Warren Hastings has often been compared with the trial of Verres, though Hastings was not only a far more capable, but a far less culpable man. Hastings, like Verres, was not punished. But the proceedings against him so fixed the attention of the nation upon the administration of India as to secure for wholesome principles of conduct a recognition which was never thereafter forgotten. The Act of 1784 in establishing a Board of Control responsible to Parliament found a means both for supervising the behaviour of officials and for taking the large political questions which arose in India out of the hands of the East India Company. This Board continued till India was placed under the direct sway of the British Crown in 1858. At the same time the appointment of Governors-General who were mostly men of wealth, and always men of rank and position at home, provided a safeguard against such misconduct as the proconsuls under the Roman Republic had been prone to commit. These latter had little to fear from prosecution when their term of office was over, and the opinion of their class was not shocked by offences which would have fatally discredited an English nobleman. The standard by which English public opinion judges the behaviour of Indian or Colonial officials has, on the whole, risen during the nineteenth century; and the idea that the government of subject-races is to be regarded as a trust to be discharged with a sense of responsibility to God and to humanity at large has become generally

[1] See Sir C. P. Ilbert's *Government of India*, p. 68. The provision creating this Court has never been repealed.

accepted. Probably the action of the Emperors, or at least of such men as Trajan and his three successors, raised the standard of opinion in the Roman Empire also. It was, however, not so much to that opinion as to their sovereign master that Roman officials were responsible. The general principles of policy which guided the Emperors were sound, but how far they were applied to check corruption or oppression in each particular case is a matter on which we are imperfectly informed. Under an indolent or vicious Emperor, a governor who had influence at Court, or who remitted the full tribute punctually, may probably have sinned with impunity.

The government of India by the English resembles that of her provinces by Rome in being virtually despotic. In both cases, whatever may have been done for the people, nothing was or is done by the people. There was under Rome, and there is in British India, no room for popular initiative, or for popular interference with the acts of the rulers, from the Viceroy down to a district official. For wrongs cognizable by the courts of law, the courts of law were and are open, doubtless more fully open in India than they were in the Roman Empire. But for errors in policy or for defects in the law itself, the people of a province had no remedy available in the Roman Empire except through petition to the sovereign. Neither is there now in India any recourse open to the inhabitants except an appeal to the Crown or to Parliament, a Parliament in which the Indian subjects of the Crown have not been, and cannot be, represented. This was, and is, by the nature of the case, inevitable.

Efforts have however been made in a wise and liberal spirit to give opportunities and means for the expression of native opinion, and for securing influence for it. In 1861 a statute authorized the addition to the three legislative councils of unofficial members to be appointed by the Governors. In 1892 power was given to certain external persons and bodies to nominate members whom the Governor might appoint, and in practice he always followed the nominations. In 1907 a system of election was introduced for other members in addition to the unofficial appointees, and the numbers in all the councils were increased [1].

In comparing the governmental systems of the two Empires, it is hardly necessary to advert to such differences as the fact that India is placed under a Viceroy to whom all the other high functionaries, Governors, Lieutenant-Governors and Chief Commissioners, are subordinated, whereas, in the Roman world every provincial governor stood directly under the Emperor. Neither need one dwell upon the position in the English system of the Secretary of State for India in Council as a member of the British Cabinet. Such details do not affect the main point to which I now come.

The territories conquered by the Romans were of three kinds. Some, such as Egypt, Macedonia, and Pontus, had been, under their own princes, monarchies practically despotic. In these, of course, there could be no question of what we call popular government. Some had been tribal principalities, monarchic or oligarchic, such as those among the Iceni and Brigantes in Britain, the Arverni in Gaul, the Cantabrian mountaineers in Spain. Here, again, free institutions had not existed before, and could hardly have been created by the conqueror. The third kind consisted of small commonwealths, such as the Greek cities. These were fitted for self-government, which indeed they had enjoyed before they had become subject to Rome. Very wisely, municipal

[1] These changes originally applied to the Governor-General's Council for all India and to those of Madras and Bombay. Now, under the Act of 1907, the elective system is in force for the Viceroy's Council and also for the legislative Councils of Madras, Bombay, Bengal, the United Provinces (Agra and Oudh) Bihar and Orissa, Punjab and Burma.

self-government was to a large extent left to them by the Emperors down till the time of Justinian. It was more complete in some cities than in others; and it was in nearly all gradually reduced by the equalizing pressure of the central authority. But they were all placed under the governor of the province; most of them paid taxes, and in most both the criminal and the higher civil jurisdiction were in the hands of imperial officials. Of the introduction of any free institutions for the Empire at large, or even for any province as a whole, there seems never to have been any question. Among the many constitutional inventions we owe to the ancient world representative government finds no place. A generation before the fall of the Republic, Rome had missed her opportunity when the creation of such a system was most needed and might have been most useful. After her struggle against the league of her Italian allies, she consented to admit them to vote in her own city tribes, instead of taking what seems to us moderns the obvious expedient of allowing them to send delegates to an assembly which should meet in Rome. So it befell that monarchy and a city republic, or confederation of city republics, remained the only political forms known to antiquity [1].

India is ruled despotically by the English, not merely because they found her so ruled, but because they con-

[1] The nearest approach to any kind of provincial self-government and also the nearest approach to a representative system was made in the Provincial Councils which seem from the time of Augustus down to the fifth century to have existed in all or nearly all the provinces. They consisted of delegates from the cities of each province, and met annually in some central place, where stood the temple or altar to Rome and Augustus. They were presided over by the priest of these divinities, and their primary functions were to offer sacrifices, provide for the expense of the annual games, and elect the priest for next year. However they seem to have also passed resolutions, such as votes of thanks to the outgoing priest or to a departing governor and to have transmitted requests or inquiries to the Emperor. Sometimes they arranged for the prosecution of a governor who had misgoverned them: but on the whole their functions were more ceremonial and ornamental than practically important; nor would the emperors have suffered them to exert any real power, though they were valued as useful vehicles of provincial opinion (see Marquardt, *Römische Staatsverwaltung*, vol. i, and an article in *Eng. Hist. Review* for April, 1893, by Mr. E. G. Hardy).

ceive that no other sort of government would suit a vast population of different races and tongues, divided by the religious animosities of Hindus and Musulmans, and with no sort of experience of self-government on a scale larger than that of the Village Council. No more in India than in the Roman Empire has there been any question of establishing free institutions either for the country as a whole, or for any particular province. But the English, like the Romans, have permitted such self-government as they found to subsist. It subsists only in the very rudimentary but very useful form of the Village Council just referred to, called in some parts of India the Panchayet or body of Five. Of late years municipal constitutions, resembling at a distance those of English boroughs, have been given to some of the larger cities, in the first instance as a sort of experiment, for the sake of training the people to a sense of public duty, and of relieving the provincial government of local duties. So far the plan has been generally justified by experience, though in some cities it has proved only a moderate success. The truth is that, though a few intelligent men, educated in European ideas, complain of the despotic power of the Anglo-Indian bureaucracy, the people of India generally do not wish to govern themselves. Their traditions, their habits, their ideas, are all the other way, and dispose them to accept submissively any rule which is strong and which neither disturbs their religion and customs nor lays too heavy imposts upon them.

Here let an interesting contrast be noted. The Roman Emperors were despots at home in Italy, almost as much, and ultimately quite as much, as in the provinces. The English govern their own country on democratic, India on absolutist principles. The inconsistency is patent but inevitable. It affords an easy theme for declamation when any arbitrary act of the Indian administration gives rise to complaints, and it may fairly be used as the foundation for an argument that a people which enjoys freedom at home is specially bound to deal justly and considerately with those subjects to whom she refuses a like freedom. But every one admits in his heart that it is impossible to ignore the differences which make one group of races unfit for the institutions which have given energy and contentment to another more favourably placed.

A similar inconsistency presses on the people of the United States in the Philippine Isles. It is a more obtrusive inconsistency because it has come more abruptly, because it has come, not by the operation of a long series of historical causes, but by the sudden and little considered action of the American Republic itself, and because the American Republic has proclaimed, far more loudly and clearly than the English have ever done, the principle contained in the Declaration of Independence that the consent of the governed is the only foundation of all just government. The Americans will doubtless in time either reconcile themselves to their illogical position or alter it. But for the present it gives to thoughtful men among them visions of mocking spirits, which the clergy are summoned to exorcize by dwelling upon the benefits which the diffusion of a pure faith and a commercial civilization may be expected to confer upon the indolent and superstitious inhabitants of these tropical isles [1].

Subject to the general principle that the power of the Emperor was everywhere supreme and absolute, the Romans recognized, at least in the earlier days of the Empire, considerable differences between the methods of administering various provinces. A distinction was drawn between the provinces of the Roman people, to which proconsuls or propraetors were sent, and the prov-

[1] Since this Essay was first published the U. S. Government have introduced an elective element into the legislature in the Philippines and have intimated their intention to extend self-government as far as may be possible under the educational and social conditions from time to time existing.

inces of Caesar, placed under the more direct control of the Emperor, and administered in his name by an official called the *praeses* or *legatus Caesaris,* or sometimes (as was the case of Judaea, at the time when it was ruled by Pontius Pilate) by a *procurator,* an officer primarily financial, but often entrusted with the powers of a *praeses.* Egypt received special treatment because the population was turbulent and liable to outbursts of religious passion, and because it was important to keep a great cornfield of the Empire in good humour. These distinctions between one province and another tended to vanish as the administrative system of the whole Empire grew better settled and the old republican forms were forgotten. Still there were always marked differences between Britain, for instance, at the one end of the realm and Syria at the other. So there were all sorts of varieties in the treatment of cities and tribes which had never been conquered, but passed peaceably through alliance into subjection. Some of the Hellenic cities retained their republican institutions till far down in imperial times. Distinctions not indeed similar, yet analogous, have existed between the different parts of British India. There is the old distribution of provinces into Regulation and Non-Regulation. The name 'Province,' one may observe in passing, a name unknown elsewhere in the dominions of Britain [1] (though a recent and somewhat vulgar usage sometimes applies it to the parts of England outside of London) except as a relic of French rule in Canada, bears witness to an authority which began, as in Canada, through conquest. Though the names of Regulation and Non-Regulation provinces are now no longer used, a distinction remains between the districts to the higher posts in which none but members of the covenanted service are ap-

[1] The use of the word to denote the two great ecclesiastical divisions of England (Province of Canterbury and Province of York) is a relic of the Roman imperial system. The application of the term to the four chief divisions of Ireland is merely popular.

pointed, and those in which the Government have a wider range of choice, and also between those districts for which the Governor-General can make ordinances in his executive capacity, and those which are legislated for by him in Council in the ordinary way. There are also many differences in the administrative systems of the different Presidencies and other territories, besides of course all imaginable diversities in the amount of independence left to the different 'Protected States,' some of which are powerful kingdoms, like Hyderabad, while many, as for instance in Gujarat, are petty principalities of two or three dozen square miles.

The mention of these Protected States suggests another point of comparison. Rome brought many principalities or kingdoms under her influence, especially in the eastern parts of the Empire; and dealt with each upon the basis of the treaty by which her supremacy had been acknowledged, allowing to some a wider, to some a narrower measure of autonomy.[1] Ultimately, however, all these, except a few on the frontiers, passed under her direct sway: and this frequently happened in cases where the native dynasty had died out, so that the title lapsed to the Emperor. The Iceni in Britain seem to have been such a protected State, and it was the failure of male heirs that caused a lapse. So the Indian Government was wont, when the ruling family became extinct or hopelessly incompetent, to annex to the dominions of the British Crown the principality it had ruled. From the days of Lord Canning, however, a new policy has been adopted. It is now deemed better to maintain the native dynasties whenever this can be done, so a childless prince is suffered to adopt, or provide for the adoption of, some person approved by the Government; and the descen-

[1] For instance, Cappadocia, Pontus, and Commagene were left as subject kingdoms till 17 A. D., 63 A. D., and 72 A. D. respectively.

dants of this person are recognized as rulers [1]. The incoming prince feels that he owes his power to the British Government, while adoption gives him a title in the eyes of his subjects.

The differences I have mentioned between the British provinces are important, not only as respects administration, but also as respects the system of landholding. All over India, as in many other Oriental countries, it is from the land that a large part of revenue, whether one calls it rent or land tax, is derived. In some provinces the rent is paid direct to the Government by the cultivator, in others it goes to intermediary landlords, who in their turn are responsible to the State. In some provinces it has been permanently fixed, by what is called a Land-settlement [2], and not always on the same principles. The subject is far too large and intricate to be pursued here. I mention it because in the Roman Empire also land revenue was the mainstay of the imperial treasury. Where territory had been taken in war, the fact of conquest was deemed to have made the Roman people ultimate owners of the land so acquired, and the cultivators became liable to pay what we should call rent for it. In some provinces this rent was farmed out to contractors called *publicani,* who offered to the State the sum equivalent to the rent of the area contracted for, minus the expense of collection and their own profit on the undertaking, and kept for themselves whatever they could extract from the peasantry. This vicious

[1] 'The extent to which confidence has been restored by Lord Canning's edict is shown by the curious fact that since its promulgation a childless ruler very rarely adopts in his own lifetime. An heir presumptive, who knows that he is to succeed and who may possibly grow restive if his inheritance is delayed, is for various obscure reasons not the kind of person whom an Oriental ruler cares to see idling about his palace, so that a politic chief often prefers leaving the duty of nominating a successor to his widows, who know his mind and have every reason for wishing him long life.'—Sir A. C. Lyall in *Law Quarterly Review* for October, 1893.

[2] One finds something similar to this Land-settlement in the Roman plan of determining the land revenue of a province by what was called the *lex provinciae.*

system, resembling that of the tithe farmers in Ireland seventy years ago, was regulated under Nero and abolished by Hadrian, who placed the imperial procurator in charge of the land revenue except as regarded the forests and mines. It exists to-day in the Ottoman Empire. Convenient as it may seem for the State, it is wasteful, and naturally exposes the peasant, as is conspicuously the case in Asiatic Turkey, to oppressions perhaps even harder to check than are those of State officials. When the English came to India they found it in force there; and the present landlord class in Bengal, called Zemindars, are the representatives of the rent or land tax-farmers under the native princes who were, perhaps unwisely, recognized as landowners by the British a century ago. This kind of tax-farming is, however, no longer practised in India, a merit to be credited to the English when we are comparing them with the Romans of the Republic and the earlier Empire.

Where the revenue of the State comes from the land, the State is obliged to keep a watchful eye upon the condition of agriculture, since revenue must needs decline when agriculture is depressed. There was not in the Roman world, and there is not in India now, any question of agricultural depression arising from foreign competition, for no grain came into the Empire from outside, or comes now into India[1]. But a year of drought, or, in a long course of years, the exhaustion of the soil, tells heavily on the agriculturist, and may render him unable to pay his rent or land tax. In bad years it was the practice of the more indulgent Emperors to remit a part of the tax for the year: and one of the complaints most frequently made against harsh sovereigns, or extravagant ones like Justinian, was that they refused to concede such remissions. A similar indulgence has to be and is granted in India in like cases.

[1] Rice, however, is sent from Lower Burma into India proper.

Finance was the standing difficulty of the Roman as it is of the Anglo-Indian administrator. Indeed, the Roman Empire may be said to have perished from want of revenue. Heavy taxation, and possibly the exhaustion of the soil, led to the abandonment of farms, reducing the rent derivable from the land. The terrible pestilence of the second century A. D. brought down population, and was followed by a famine. The eastern provinces had never furnished good fighting material: and the diminution of the agricultural population of Italy, due partly to this cause, partly to the growth of large estates worked by slave labour, made it necessary to recruit the armies from the barbarians on the frontiers. Even in the later days of the Republic the native auxiliaries were beginning to be an important part of a Roman army. Moreover, with a declining revenue, a military establishment such as was needed to defend the eastern and the northern frontiers could not always be maintained. The Romans had no means of drawing a revenue from frontier customs, because there was very little import trade; but dues were levied at ports and there was a succession tax, which usually stood at five per cent. In most provinces there were few large fortunes on which an income or property tax could have been levied, except those of persons who were already paying up to their capacity, as being responsible for the land tax assessed upon their districts. The tax on salt was felt so sorely by the poor that Aurelian was hailed as a benefactor when he abolished it.

India has for many years past been, if not in financial straits, yet painfully near the limit of her taxable resources. The salt tax used to press hard upon the peasant, but it has been of late years reduced and is now less than a farthing (half a cent) per pound. And the number of fortunes from which much can be extracted by an income or property tax is very small in proportion to the population, because the rents of agricultural land are exempted. Comparing her total wealth with her population, India is a poor country, probably poorer than was the Roman Empire in the time of Constantine[1]. A heavy burden lies upon her in respect of the salaries of the upper branches of the Civil Service, which must be fixed at figures sufficient to attract a high order of talent from England, for it is essential to secure such talent for the very difficult and responsible work assigned to these officials. Still heavier is the burden in respect of military charges. On the other hand, India has the advantage of being able, when the guarantee of the British Government is given for the loan, to borrow money for railways and other public works, at a rate of interest very low as compared with what the best Native State would be obliged to offer, or as compared with that which the Roman Government had to pay.

Under the Republic, Rome levied tribute from the provinces, and spent some of it on herself, though of course the larger part went to the general expenses of the military and civil administration. Under the Emperors that which was spent in Rome became gradually less and less, as the Emperor became more and more detached from the imperial city, and after Diocletian, Italy was treated as a province. England, like Spain in the days of her American Empire and like Holland now, for a time drew from her Indian conquests a substantial revenue. An inquiry made in 1773 showed that, since 1765, about two millions a year had been paid by the Company to the British exchequer. By 1773, however,

[1] The total gross revenue of British India was in 1840 200,000,000 rupees, and in 1910-11 had risen to 1,204,893,500 rupees, about one-fourth of which was land revenue and about one-third derived from railways. The land revenue is somewhat increasing with the bringing under cultivation of additional land. It is estimated that forty-two per cent. of the cultivated area is available for improved cultivation. A sum of £331,000,000 has been expended upon railways in British India and the Protected Native States. The total permanent debt now stands at £266,000,000, and the temporary debt at about £9,000,000.

the Company had incurred such heavy debts that the exchequer had to lend them money: and since that time Britain has drawn no tribute from India. She profits by her dominion only in respect of having an enormous market for her goods, industrial or commercial enterprises offering comparatively safe investments for her capital, and a field where her sons can make a career. Apart from any considerations of justice or of sentiment, India could not afford to make any substantial contribution to the expenses of the non-Indian dominions of the Crown. It is all she can do to pay her own way, and if the revenue could be increased by raising taxation further, there are many Indian objects, such as education and sanitation, on which the Government would gladly spend more money.

Those whom Rome sent out to govern the provinces were, in the days of the Republic and in the days of Augustus, Romans, that is to say Roman citizens and natives of Italy. Very soon, however, citizens born in the provinces began to be admitted to the great offices and to be selected by the Emperor for high employment. As early as the time of Nero, an Aquitanian chief, Julius Vindex, was legate of the great province of Gallia Lugdunensis. When the imperial throne itself was filled by provincials, as was often the case from Trajan onwards, it was plain that the pre-eminence of Italy was gone. If a man, deemed otherwise eligible, did not happen to be a full Roman citizen, the Emperor forthwith made him one. By the time of the Antonines (A. D. 138-180) there was practically no distinction between a Roman and a provincial citizen; and we may safely assume that the large majority of important posts, both military and civil, were held by men of provincial extraction. Indeed merit probably won its way faster to military than to civil distinction, for in governments which are militant as well as military, promotion by merit is essential to the success of the national arms, and the soldier identifies himself with the power he serves even faster than does the civilian. So, long before full citizenship was granted to all the inhabitants of the Roman world (about A. D. 217), it is clear that not only the lower posts in which provincials had already been employed, but the highest also were freely open to all subjects. A Gaul might be sent to govern Cilicia, or a Thracian Britain, because both were now Romans rather than Gauls or Thracians. The fact that Latin and Greek were practically familiar to nearly all highly educated civil servants, because Latin was the language of law as well as the tongue commonly spoken in the West, while Greek was the language of philosophy and (to a great extent) of letters, besides being the spoken tongue of most parts of the East, made a well-educated man fit for public employment everywhere, for he was not (except perhaps in Syria and Egypt and a few odd corners of the Empire) obliged to learn any fresh language. And a provincial was just as likely as an Italian to be highly educated. Thus the officials could easily get into touch with the subjects, and felt hardly more strange if they came from a distance than a Scotchman feels if he is appointed to a professorship in Quebec, or an Irishman if he becomes postmaster in a Norfolk village. Nothing contributed more powerfully to the unity and the strength of the Roman dominion than this sense of an imperial nationality.

The English in India have, as did the Romans, always employed the natives in subordinate posts. The enormous majority of persons who carry on the civil administration there at this moment are Asiatics. But the English, unlike the Romans, have continued to reserve the higher posts for men of European stock. The contrast in this respect between the Roman and the English policy is instructive, and goes down to the foundation of the differences between English and Roman rule. As we have seen, the City of Rome became the Empire, and the Empire became Rome. National independence was not regretted, for the East had been denationalized before the Italian conqueror appeared, and the tribes of the West, even those who fought best for freedom, had not reached a genuine national life when Spain, Gaul, and Britain were brought under the yoke. In the third century A. D. a Gaul, a Spaniard, a Pannonian, a Bithynian, a Syrian called himself a Roman, and for all practical purposes was a Roman. The interests of the Empire were his interests, its glory his glory, almost as much as if he had been born in the shadow of the Capitol. There was, therefore, no reason why his loyalty should not be trusted, no reason why he should not be chosen to lead in war, or govern in peace, men of Italian birth. So, too, the qualities which make a man capable of leading in war or administering in peace were just as likely to be found in a Gaul, or a Spaniard, or a German from the Rhine frontier as in an Italian. In fact, men of Italian birth play no great part in later imperial history [1].

It is far otherwise in India, though there was among the races of India no nation. The Englishman does not become an Indian, nor the Indian an Englishman. The Indian does not as a rule, though of course there have been not a few remarkable exceptions to the rule, possess the qualities which the English deem to be needed for leadership in war or for the higher posts of administration in peace [2]. For several reasons, reasons to be referred to later, he can seldom be expected to feel like an Englishman, and to have that full comprehension of the principles of British policy which may be counted on in an Englishman. Accordingly the English have

[1] After the fifth century, Armenians, Isaurians, and Northern Macedonians figure more largely in the Eastern Empire than do natives of the provinces round the Aegean.

[2] Among these exceptions may be mentioned Sir Syed Ahmed of Aligurh, and the late Mr. Justice Trimbak Telang of Bombay, both men of remarkable width of view and force of character.

made in India arrangements to which there was nothing similar in the Roman Empire. They have two armies, a native and a European, the latter of which is never suffered to fall below a certain ratio to the former. The latter is composed entirely of Englishmen. In the former all military posts in line regiments above that of subahdar (equivalent to captain) are reserved to Englishmen [1]. The artillery and engineer services are kept in English hands, *i. e.* there is hardly any native artillery. It is only, therefore, in the native contingents already referred to that natives are found in the higher grades. These contingents may be compared with the auxiliary barbarian troops under non-Roman commanders whom we find in the later ages of Rome, after Constantine. Such commanders proved sometimes, like the Vandal Stilicho, energetic defenders of the imperial throne, sometimes, like the Suevian Ricimer, formidable menaces to it [2]. But apart from these, the Romans had but one army; and it was an army in which all subjects had an equal chance of rising.

In a civil career, the native of India may go higher under the English than he can in a military one. A few natives, mostly Hindus, and indeed largely Bengali Hindus, have won their way into the civil service by passing the competitive Indian Civil Service examination in England, and some of these have risen to the posts of magistrate, of revenue commissioner, and of district judge. A fair proportion of the seats on the benches of the Supreme Courts in Calcutta, Madras, Bombay, Allahabad, and Lahore have been allotted to native barristers of eminence, several of whom have shown them-

[1] The subahdar, however, is rather a non-commissioned than a commissioned officer, and is not a member of the British officers' mess.

[2] Russia places Musulmans from the Caucasian provinces in high military posts. But she has no army corresponding to the native army in India, and as she has a number of Musulman subjects in European Russia it has been all the more natural for her to have a Colonel Temirhan Shipsheff at Aralykh and a General Alikhanoff at Merv.

selves equal in point of knowledge and capacity, as well as in integrity, to the best judges selected from the European bar in India or sent out from the English bar. A native Indian now (1913) holds the important post of legal member of the Viceroy's Executive Council, and there are native members on the Executive Councils of Madras, Bombay, and Bengal. No native, however seems to have been as yet seriously considered for the very highest places, such as those of Lieutenant-Governor or Chief Commissioner, although all British subjects are legally eligible for any post in the service of the Crown in any part of the British Dominions.

Regarding the policy of this exclusion there has been much difference of opinion. As a rule, Anglo-Indian officials approve the course which I have described as that actually taken. But I know some who think that there are natives of ability and force of character such as to fit them for posts military as well as civil, higher than any to which a native has yet been advanced, and who see advantages in selecting a few for such posts. They hold, however, that such natives ought to be selected for civil appointments, not by competitive examination in England but in India itself by those who rule there, and in respect of their special personal merits tested by service. Some opposition to such a method might be expected from members of the regular civil service, who would consider their prospects of promotion to be thereby prejudiced.

Here we touch an extremely interesting point of comparison between the Roman and the English systems. Both nations, when they started on their career of conquest, had already built up at home elaborate constitutional systems in which the rights of citizens, both public and private civil rights, had been carefully settled and determined. What was the working of these rights in the conquered territories? How far were they extended to the new subjects by the conquerors, Roman and English, and with what results?

Rome set out from the usual practice of the city republics of the ancient world, in which no man enjoyed any rights at all, public or private, except a citizen of the Republic. A stranger coming to reside in the city did not, no matter how long he lived there nor did his son or grandson, obtain those rights unless he was specially admitted to become a citizen. From this principle Rome, as she grew, presently found herself obliged to deviate. She admitted one set of neighbours after another, sometimes as allies, sometimes in later days, as conquered and incorporated communities, to a citizenship which was sometimes incomplete, including only private civil rights, sometimes complete, including the right of voting in the assembly and the right of being chosen to a public office. Before the dictatorship of Julius Caesar practically all Italians, except the people of Cisalpine Gaul, which remained a province till B. C. 43, had been admitted to civic rights. Citizenship, complete or partial (*i. e.* including or not including public rights), had also begun to be conferred on a certain number of cities or individuals outside Italy. Tarsus in Cilicia, of which St. Paul was a native, enjoyed it, so he was born a Roman citizen. This process of enlarging citizenship went on with accelerated speed, in and after the days of the Flavian Emperors. Under Hadrian, the whole of Spain seems to have enjoyed civic rights. Long before this date the ancient right of voting in the Roman popular Assembly had become valueless, but the other advantages attached to the status of citizen were worth having, for they secured valuable immunities. Finally, early in the third century A. D., every Roman subject was by imperial edict made a citizen for all purposes whatsoever. Universal eligibility to office had, as we have seen, gone ahead of this extension, for all offices lay in the gift of the Emperor or his ministers; and when it was desired to appoint any one who might not be a full citizen, citizenship was conferred along with the office. Thus Rome at last extended to all her subjects the rights that had originally been confined to her own small and exclusive community.

In England itself, the principle that all private civil rights belong to every subject alike was very soon established, and may be said to have never been doubted since the final extinction of serfdom in the beginning of the seventeenth century. Public civil rights, however, did not necessarily go with private. Everybody, it is true, was (subject to certain religious restrictions now almost entirely repealed) eligible to any office to which he might be appointed by the Crown, and was also (subject to certain property qualifications which lasted till our own time) capable of being chosen to fill any elective post or function, such as that of member of the House of Commons. But the right of voting did not necessarily go along with other rights, whether public or private, and it is only within the last forty years that it has been extended by a series of statutes to the bulk of the adult male population. Now, when Englishmen began to settle abroad, they carried with them all their private rights as citizens, and also their eligibility to office; but their other public rights, *i. e.* those of voting, they could not carry, because these were attached to local areas in England. When territories outside England were conquered, their free inhabitants, in becoming subjects of the Crown, became therewith entitled to all such rights of British subjects as were not connected with residence in Britain: that is to say, they had all the private civil rights of Englishmen, and also complete eligibility to public office (unless of course some special disqualification was imposed). The rights of an English settler in Massachusetts in the seventeenth and eighteenth centuries were those of an Englishman, except that he could not vote at an English parliamentary election because he was not resident in any English constituency; and the same rule became applicable to a French Canadian after the cession of Canada to the British Crown.

When India was conquered, the same principles were again applied. Every free Indian subject of the Crown soon became entitled to the private civil rights of an Englishman, except so far as his own personal law, Hindu or Musulman or Parsi or Jain, might modify those rights; and if there was any such modification, that was recognized for his benefit rather than to his prejudice. Thus the process which the Romans took centuries to complete was effected almost at once in India by the application of long established doctrines of English law. Accordingly we have in India the singular result that although there are in that country no free institutions (other than those municipal ones previously referred to) nor any representative government, every Indian subject is eligible to any office in the gift of the Crown anywhere, and to any post or function to which any body of electors may select him. He may be chosen by a British constituency a member of the British House of Commons. Two natives of India (both Parsis) have already been chosen, both by London constituencies, to sit in the British House. So a native Hindu or Musulman might be appointed by the Crown to be Lord Chief Justice of England or Governor-General of Canada or Australia. He might be created a peer. He might become Prime Minister. And as far as mere legal eligibility goes, he might be named Governor-General of India. Neither birth, nor colour, nor religion constitutes any legal disqualification. This was expressly declared as regards India by the India Act of 1833, and has been more than once formally declared since, but it did not require any statute to establish what flowed from the principles of British law. And it need hardly be added that the same principles apply to the Chinese subjects of the Crown in Hong Kong or Singapore, to the Kafir subjects of the Crown in Zululand, to the Red Indian subjects of the Crown in British Columbia, and to the Maori subjects of the Crown in New Zealand. In this respect at least England has worthily repeated the liberal policy of Rome. She has done it, however, not by way of special grants, but by the automatic and probably uncontemplated operation of the general principles of her law.

As I have referred to the influence of English constitutional ideas, it is worth noting that it is these ideas and the extension of democratic principles in Britain and her colonies that have led the English of late years not only to create in India city municipalities, things entirely foreign to the native Indian mind, but also to provide by statute (see above, p. 43) for the admission of non-official members—some nominated, some elected—to the legislative council of the Viceroy and to the provincial councils above referred to. The admission of such native members who are independent of governmental influences testifies to the wish of the Government to let native opinion have free expression and to submit its own acts and declarations of policy to the ordeal of public debate. In the Roman Empire such an expedient was not needed for the purpose of bridging the chasm between rulers and ruled, for the former class came out of the latter class. For the purpose of securing a free criticism of provincial administration it would have been helpful, but the imperial government desired no such criticism.

The extension of the civil rights of Englishmen to the subjects of the Crown in India would have been anything but a boon had it meant the degradation or extinction of native law and custom. This of course it has not meant. Neither had the extension of Roman conquest such an effect in the Roman Empire; and even the grant of citizenship to all subjects did not quite efface local law and usage. As the position and influence of English law in India, viewed in comparison with the relation of the older Roman law to the Roman provinces, is treated of in the next following Essay, I will here pass over the legal side of the matter, and speak only of the parallel to be noted between the political action of the conquering nations in both cases.

Both have shown a prudent wish to avoid disturbing, any further than the fixed principles of their policy made needful, the usages and beliefs of their subjects. The Romans took over the social and political system which they found in each of the very dissimilar regions they conquered, placed their own officials above it, modified it so far as they found expedient for purposes of revenue and civil administration generally, but otherwise let it stand as they found it and left the people alone. In course of time the law and administration of the conquerors, and the intellectual influences which literature called into play, did bring about a considerable measure of assimilation between Romans and provincials, especially as respected the life and ideas of the upper classes. But this was the result of natural causes. The Romans did not consciously and deliberately work for uniformity. Especially in the sphere of religion did they abstain from all interference. They had indeed no temptation to interfere either with religious belief or with religious practice, for their own original worship was not a universal but a strictly national religion, and the educated classes had begun to sit rather loose to that religion before the process of foreign conquest had gone far. According to the theory of the ancient world, every nation had its own deities, and all these deities were equally to be respected each in their own country. Whether they were at bottom the same deities under different names, or were quite independent divine powers, did not matter. Every nation and every member of a nation was expected to worship the national gods; but so long as an individual man did not openly reject or insult those gods, he might if he pleased worship a god belonging to some other country, provided that the worship was not conducted with shocking or demoralizing rites, such as had in republican days led to the prohibition of the Bacchanalian cult at Rome [1]. The Egyptian Serapis was a fashionable deity among Roman women as early as the time of Catullus. We are told that Claudius abolished Druidism on account of its savage cruelty, but this may mean no more than that he forbade the Druidic practice of human sacrifices [2]. There was therefore, speaking broadly, no religious persecution and little religious intolerance in the ancient world, for the Christians, it need hardly be said, were persecuted not because of their religion but because they were deemed to constitute a secret society, about which, since it was new, and secret, and Oriental, and rejected all the gods of all the nations alike, the wildest calumnies were readily believed. The first government to set the example of a genuinely religious persecution seems to have been that of the Persian Fire-worshipping kings of the Sassanid dynasty, who occasionally worried their Christian subjects.

Neither, broadly speaking, was religious propagandism known to the ancient world. There were no missions, neither foreign missions nor home missions. If a man did not sacrifice to the gods of his own country, his fellow citizens might think ill of him. If he was accused of teaching that the gods did not exist, he might possibly, like Socrates, be put to death as a dangerous mem-

[1] Constantine prohibited the immoral excesses practised by the Syrians of Heliopolis.

[2] 'Druidarum religionem apud Gallos dirae immanitatis et tantum civibus sub Augusto interdictam penitus abolevit.'—Sueton, *Vita Claud.* c. 25.

ber of society, but nobody sought by preaching or otherwise to reclaim him from error. On the other hand, if he did worship the nation's gods, he was in the right path, and it would have been deemed not only impertinent, but almost impious, for the native of another country to seek to convert him to another faith, that is to say, to make him disloyal to the gods of his own country, who were its natural and time-honoured protectors. The only occasions on which one hears of people being required to perform acts of worship to any power but the deities of their country are those cases in which travellers were expected to offer a prayer or a sacrifice to some local deity whose territory they were traversing, and whom it was therefore expedient to propitiate, and those other cases in which a sort of worship was required to be rendered by subjects to the monarch, or to the special protecting deity of the monarch, under whose sway they lived. The edict attributed to Nebuchadnezzar in the book of Daniel may in this connexion be compared with the practice in the Roman Empire of adoring the spirit that watched over the reigning Caesar. To burn incense on the altar of the Genius of the Emperor was the test commonly proposed to the persons accused of being Christians.

All this is the natural result of polytheism. With the coming of faiths each of which claims to be exclusively and universally true, the face of the world was changed. Christianity was necessarily a missionary religion, and unfortunately presently became also, forgetting the precepts of its Founder, a persecuting religion. Islam followed in the same path, and for similar reasons. In India the strife of Hinduism with Buddhists and Jains gave rise to ferocious persecutions, which however were perhaps as much political as religious. When the Portuguese and Spaniards began to discover and conquer new countries beyond the oceans, the spread of religion was in the mouths of all the adventurers, and an object of real moment in the minds of many of the baser as well as of the better sort. Spain accordingly forced her faith upon all her subjects, and found no great resistance from the aboriginal native American peoples, though of course their Christianity seldom went deep, as indeed it remains to-day in many parts of Central and South America, a thin veneer over the ancient superstitions. Portugal did the like, so far as she could, in India and in Africa. So too the decrees by which the French colonizing companies were founded in the days of Richelieu provided that the Roman Catholic faith was to be everywhere made compulsory, and that converted pagans were to be admitted to the full civil rights of Frenchmen [1]. But when the English set forth to trade and afterwards to conquer in India they were not thinking of religion at all. The middle of the eighteenth century, when Bengal and Madras were acquired, was for England an age when persecution had died out and missionary propagandism had scarcely begun. The East India Company did not at first interfere in any way with the religious rites it found practised by the people, however cruel or immoral they might be. It gave no advantages to Christian converts, and for a good while it even discouraged the presence of missionaries, lest they should provoke disturbances. Bishops were thought less dangerous, and one was appointed, with three Archdeacons under him, by the Act of 1813. A sort of miniature church establishment, for the benefit of Europeans, still exists in India and is supported out of Indian revenues. After a time, however, some of the more offensive or harmful features of native worship began to be forbidden. The human sacrifices that occasionally occurred among the hill tribes were

[1] I owe this fact to Sir A. C. Lyall (*op. cit.* p. 66). But it does not appear that in practice the French tried to force the Red Indians into Christianity. They had difficulties enough without adding that.

treated as murders, and the practice of Sutti—the self-immolation of the Hindu widow on her husband's funeral pyre—was forbidden as far back as 1829. No hindrance is now thrown in the way of Christian missions: and there is perfect equality, as respects civil rights and privileges, not only between the native votaries of different native religions, but also between them and Europeans.

So far as religion properly so-called is concerned, the policy of the English is simple and easy to apply. But as respects usages which are more or less associated with religion in the native mind, but which European sentiment disapproves, difficulties sometimes arise. The burning of the widow was one of these usages, and has been dealt with at the risk of offending Hindu prejudice. Infanticide is another; and the British Government try to check it, even in some of the protected States. The marriage of young children is a third: and this it has been thought not yet prudent to forbid, although the best native opinion is beginning to recognize the evils that attach to it. Speaking generally, it may be said that the English have, like the Romans but unlike the Spaniards, shown their desire to respect the customs and ideas of the conquered peoples. Indifferentism has served them in their career of conquest as well as religious eclecticism served the Romans, so that religious sentiment, though it sometimes stimulated the valour of their native enemies, has not really furnished any obstacle to the pacification of a conquered people. The English have, however, gone further than did the Romans in trying to deter their subjects from practices socially or morally deleterious.

As regards the work done by the English for education in the establishment of schools and universities, no comparison with Rome can usefully be drawn, because it was not deemed in the ancient world to be the function of the State to make a general educational provision for its subjects. The Emperors, however, appointed and paid teachers of the liberal arts in some of the greater cities. That which the English have done, however, small as it may appear in comparison with the vast population they have to care for [1], witnesses to the spirit which has animated them in seeking to extend to the conquered the opportunities of progress which they value for themselves. Their wish to diffuse education has been limited in practice only by financial considerations.

The question how far the triumphs of Rome and of England are due to the republican polity of the one, and the practically republican (though not until 1867 or 1885 democratic) polity of the other, is so large a one that I must be content merely to indicate it as well deserving a discussion. Several similar empires have been built up by republican governments of the oligarchic type, as witness the empire of Carthage in the ancient, and that of Venice in the later mediaeval world. One can explain this by the fact that in such governments there is usually, along with a continuity of policy hardly to be expected from a democracy, a constant succession of capable generals and administrators such as a despotic hereditary monarchy seldom provides, for a monarchy of that kind must from time to time have feeble or dissolute sovereigns, under whom bad selections will be made for important posts, policy will oscillate, and no adequate support will be given to the armies or fleets which are maintaining the interests of the nation abroad. A republic is moreover likely to have a larger stock of capable and experienced men on which to draw during the process of conquering and organizing. The two conspicuous instances in which

[1] There are in India five examining and degree-granting Universities, with about (in 1912) 30,000 matriculated students, nearly all of them taught in the numerous affiliated colleges. The total number of persons returned as receiving instruction in British India is 6,212,000, of whom 831,000 are girls.

monarchies have acquired and long held vast external dominions are the Empires of Spain and Russia. The former case is hardly an exception to the doctrine just stated, because the oceanic Empire of Spain was won quickly and with little fighting against opponents immeasurably inferior, and because it had no conterminous enemies in the western hemisphere to take advantage of the internal decay which soon set in [2]. In the case of Russia the process has been largely one of natural expansion over regions so thinly peopled and with inhabitants so backward that no serious resistance was made to an advance which went on rather by settlement than by conquest. Until she found herself opposed by Japan in Manchuria it was only in the Caucasus and in Turkistan that Russia had had to establish her power by fighting. Her conflicts even with the Persians and the Ottoman Turks have been, as Moltke is reported to have said, battles of the one-eyed against the blind. But it must be added that Russia has shown during two centuries a remarkable power of holding a steady course of foreign policy. She sometimes trims her sails, and lays the ship upon the other tack, but the main direction of the vessel's course is not altered. This must be the result of wisdom or good fortune in the choice of ministers, for the Romanoff dynasty has not contained more than its fair average of men of governing capacity.

There is one other point in which the Romans and the English may be compared as conquering powers. Both triumphed by force of character. During the two centuries that elapsed between the destruction of Carthage, when Rome had already come to rule many provinces, and the time of Vespasian, when she had ceased to be a city, and was passing into a nation conterminous with her dominions, the Romans were the ruling race of

[2] The wars with Portugal on the frontier of Brazil and of the region which is now Argentina and Uruguay form an exception hardly worth noting.

the world, small in numbers, even if we count all the inhabitants of middle Italy as Romans, but gifted with such talents for war and government, and possessed of such courage and force of will as to be able, not only to dominate the whole civilized world and hold down its peoples, but also to carry on a succession of bloody civil wars among themselves without giving those peoples any chance of recovering their freedom. The Roman armies, though superior in discipline to the enemies they had to encounter, except the Macedonians and Greeks, were not generally superior in weapons, and had no resources of superior scientific knowledge at their command. Their adversaries in Africa, in Greece, and in Asia Minor were as far advanced in material civilization as they were themselves. It was their strenuous and indomitable will, buoyed up by the pride and self-confidence born of a long succession of victories in the past, that enabled them to achieve this unparalleled triumph. The triumph was a triumph of character, as their poet felt when he penned the famous lines, *Moribus antiquis stat res Romana virisque.* And after the inhabitants of the City had ceased to be the heart of the Empire, this consciousness of greatness passed to the whole population of the Roman world when they compared themselves with the barbarians outside their frontiers. One finds it even in the pages of Procopius, a Syrian writing in Greek, after the western half of the Empire had been dismembered by barbarian invasions.

The English conquered India with forces much smaller than those of the Romans; and their success in subjugating a still vaster population in a shorter time may thus appear more brilliant. But the English had antagonists immeasurably inferior in valour, in discipline, in military science, and generally also in the material of war, to those whom the Romans overcame. Nor had they ever either a first-rate general or a monarch of persistent energy opposed to them. No Hannibal, nor even a Mithradates, appeared to bar their path. Hyder Ali had no nation behind him; and fortune spared them an encounter with the Afghan Ahmed Shah and the Sikh Ranjit Singh. Their most formidable opponents might rather be compared with the gallant but untrained Celtic Vercingetorix, or the showy but incompetent Antiochus the Great. It was only when Europeans like Dupleix came upon the scene that they had men of their own kind to grapple with; and Dupleix had not the support from home which Clive could count on in case of dire necessity. Still the conquest of India was a splendid achievement, more striking and more difficult, if less romantic, than the conquest of Mexico by Hernan Cortez or the conquest of Peru by Francisco Pizarro, though it must be admitted that the courage of those two adventurers in venturing far into unknown regions with a handful of followers has never been surpassed. Among the English, as among the Romans, the sense of personal force, the conscious ascendency of a race so often already victorious, with centuries of fame behind them, and a contempt for the feebler folk against whom they were contending, were the main source of that dash and energy and readiness to face any odds which bore down all resistance. These qualities have lasted into our own time. No more brilliant examples were ever given of them than in the defence of the Fort at Lucknow and in the siege of Delhi at the time of the Indian Mutiny of 1857-8. And it is worth noting that almost the only disasters that have ever befallen the British arms have occurred where the general in command was either incompetent, as must sometimes happen in every army, or was wanting in boldness. In the East, more than anywhere else, confidence makes for victory, and one victory leads on to another.

It is by these qualities that the English continue to

hold India. In the higher grades of the civil administration which they fill there are only about twelve hundred persons[1]: and these twelve hundred control three hundred and fifteen millions, doing it with so little friction that they have ceased to be surprised at this extraordinary fact. The English have impressed the imagination of the people by their resistless energy and their almost uniform success. Their domination seems to have about it an element of the supernatural, for the masses of India are still in that mental condition which looks to the supernatural for an explanation of whatever astonishes it. The British Raj fills them with a sense of awe and mystery. That over three hundred millions of men should be ruled by a few palefaced strangers from beyond the great and wide sea, strangers who all obey some distant power, and who never, like the lieutenants of Oriental sovereigns, try to revolt for their own benefit—this seems too wonderful to be anything but the doing of some unseen and irresistible divinity. I heard at Lahore an ancedote which, slight as it is, illustrates the way in which the native thinks of these things. A tiger had escaped from the Zoological Gardens, and its keeper, hoping to lure it back, followed it. When all other inducements had failed, he lifted up his voice and solemnly adjured it in the name of the British Government, to which it belonged, to come back to its cage. The tiger obeyed.

Now that we have rapidly surveyed the more salient points of resemblance or analogy between these two empires, it remains to note the capital differences between them, one or two of which have been already incidentally mentioned. On the most obvious of all I

[1] The Indian Civil Service recruited by open competition in England consisted (in 1911) of about 1250 members, of whom 65 are Indians. The entire European element in the whole civil administration is represented by less than seven thousand persons. See *Peoples and Problems of India*, by Sir W. T. Holderness, a singularly clear and instructive little book.

have already dwelt. It is the fact that, whereas the Romans conquered right out from their City in all directions—south, north, west, and east—so that the capital, during the five centuries from B. C. 200 (end of the Second Punic War) to A. D. 325 (foundation of Constantinople), stood not far from the centre of their dominions, England has conquered India across the ocean, and remains many thousands of miles from the nearest point of her Indian territory. Another not less obvious difference is perhaps less important than it seems. Rome was a city, and Britain is a country. Rome, when she stepped outside Italy to establish in Sicily her first province, had a free population of possibly only seventy or eighty thousand souls. Britain, when she began her career of conquest at Plassy, had (if we include Ireland, then still a distinct kingdom, but then less a source of weakness than she has sometimes since been) a population of at least eleven or twelve millions. But, apart from the fact that the distance from Britain to India round the Cape made her larger population less available for action in India than was the smaller population of Rome for action in the Mediterranean, the comparison must not really be made with Rome as a city, but with Rome as the centre of a large Italian population, upon which she drew for her armies, and the bulk of which had, before the end of the Republic, become her citizens. On this point of dissimilarity no more need be said, because its significance is apparent. I turn from it to another of greater consequence.

The relations of the conquering country to the conquered country, and of the conquering race to the conquered races, are totally different in the two cases compared. In the case of Rome there was a similarity of conditions which pointed to and ultimately effected a fusion of the peoples. In the case of England there is a dissimilarity which makes the fusion of her people with the peoples of India impossible.

Climate offers the first point of contrast. Rome, to be sure, ruled countries some of which were far hotter and others far colder than was the valley of the Tiber. Doubtless the officer who was stationed in Nubia complained of the torrid summer, much as an English officer complains of Quetta or Multan; nor were the winters of Ardoch or Hexham agreeable to a soldier from Apulia. But if the Roman married in Nubia, he could bring up his family there. An English officer cannot do this at Quetta or Multan. The English race becomes so enfeebled in the second generation by living without respite under the Indian sun that it would probably die out, at least in the plains, in the third or fourth generation. Few Englishmen feel disposed to make India their home, if only because the physical conditions of life there are so different from those under which their earlier years were passed. But the Italian could make himself at home, so far as natural conditions went, almost anywhere from the Dnieper to the Guadalquivir.

The second contrast is in the colour of the races. All the races of India are dark, though individuals may be found among high-caste Brahmins and among the Parsis of Poona or Gujarat who are as light in hue as many Englishmen. Now to the Teutonic peoples, and especially to the English and Anglo-Americans, the difference of colour means a great deal. It creates a feeling of separation, perhaps even of a slight repulsion. Such a feeling may be deemed unreasonable or unchristian, but it seems too deeply rooted to be effaceable in any time we can foresee. It is, to be sure, not nearly so strong towards members of the more civilized races of India, with their faces often full of an intelligence and refinement which witness to many generations of mental culture, as it is in North America towards the negroes of the Gulf Coast, or in South Africa towards the Kafirs. Yet it is sufficient to be, as a rule, a bar to social intimacy, and a complete bar to intermarriage.

Among the highest castes of Hindus and among the most ancient princely families, such as those famous Rajput dynasties whose lineage runs back further than does that of any of the royal houses of Europe, there is a corresponding pride of race quite as strong as that felt by the best-born European. So, too, some of the oldest Musulman families, tracing their origin to the relatives of the Prophet himself, are in respect of long descent equal to any European houses. Nevertheless, although the more educated and tactful among the English pay due honour to these families, colour would form an insurmountable barrier to intermarriage, even were the pride of the Rajputs disposed to invite it. The oldest of the Rajput dynasties, that of Udaipur, always refused to give a daughter in marriage even to the Mogul Emperors.

There was no severing line like this in the ancient world. The only dark races (other than the Egyptians) with whom the Romans came in contact were some of the Numidian tribes, few of whom became really Romanized, and the Nubians of the Middle Nile, also scarcely within the pale of civilization. The question, therefore, did not arise in the form it has taken in India. Probably, however, the Romans would have felt and acted not like Teutons, but rather as the Spanish and Portuguese have done. Difference of colour does not repel members of these last-named nations. Among them, unions, by which I mean legal unions, of whites with dark-skinned people, are not uncommon, nor is the mulatto or quadroon offspring kept apart and looked down upon as he is among the Anglo-Americans. Nothing contributed more to the fusion of the races and nationalities that composed the Roman Empire than the absence of any physical and conspicuous distinctions between those races, just as nothing did more to mitigate the horrors of slavery than the fact that the slave was usually of a tint and type of features not markedly unlike those of his master. Before the end of the Republic there were many freedmen in the Senate, though their presence there was regarded as a sign of declension. The son of a man who had once been a slave passed naturally and easily—as did the poet Horace—into the best society of Rome when his personal merits or the favour of a great patron gave him entrance, though his detractors found pleasure in reminding one another of his origin. In India it is otherwise. Slavery, which was never harsh there, has fortunately not come into the matter, in the way it did in the Southern States of America and in South Africa. But the population is sharply divided into whites and natives. The so-called Eurasians, a mixed race due to the unions of whites with persons of Indian race, give their sympathies to the whites, but are treated by the latter as an inferior class. They are not numerous enough to be an important factor, nor do they bridge over the chasm which divides the rulers from the ruled. It is not of the want of political liberty that the latter complain, for political liberty has never been enjoyed in the East, and would not have been dreamt of had not English literature and English college teaching implanted the idea in the minds of the educated natives. But the hauteur of the English and the sense of social incompatibility which both elements feel, are unfortunate features in the situation, and have been so from the first. Even in 1813 the representatives of the East India Company stated to a committee of the House of Commons that 'Englishmen of classes not under the observation of the supreme authorities were notorious for the contempt with which, in their ignorance and arrogance, they contemplated the usages and institutions of the natives, and for their frequent disregard of justice and humanity in their dealings with the people of India [1].' And the Act of 1833 requires the Government of India 'to provide for the protection of the natives from insult and outrage in their persons, religions, and opinions [2].'

It may be thought that, even if colour did not form an obstacle to intermarriage, religion would. Religion, however, can be changed, and colour cannot. In North America blacks and whites belong to the same religious denominations, but the social demarcation remains complete. Still it is true that the difference of religion does constitute in India a further barrier not merely to intermarriage but also to intimate social relations. Among the Musulmans the practice, or at any rate the legal possibility of polygamy, naturally deters white women from a union they might otherwise have contemplated. (There have, however, been a few instances of such unions.) Hinduism stands much further away from Christianity than does Islam; and its ceremonial rules regarding the persons in whose company food may be partaken of operate against a form of social intercourse which cements intimacy among Europeans [3].

One must always remember that in the East religion constitutes a bond of union far stronger than it does in Western Europe. It largely replaces that national feeling which is absent in India and among the Eastern peoples (except the Chinese and Japanese) generally. Among Hindus and Musulmans religious practices are inwoven with a man's whole life, and religious differences are fundamental. To the Hindu more especially caste is everything. It creates a sort of nation-

[1] See Sir C. P. Ilbert: *Government of India*, p. 77. [2] Ibid. p. 91.

[3] The number of Hindus in all India is estimated at 218 millions, that of Musulmans at 67 millions, aboriginal races ten millions, Christians nearly four millions.

ality within a nationality, dividing the man of one caste from the man of another, as well as from the man who stands outside Hinduism altogether. Among Muslims there is indeed no regular caste (though evident traces of it remain among the Muhamadans of India); but the haughty exclusiveness of Islam keeps its votaries quite apart from the professors of other faiths. The European in India, when he converses with either a Hindu or a Musulman, feels strongly how far away from them he stands. There is always a sense of constraint, because both parties know that a whole range of subjects lies outside discussion, and must not be even approached. It is very different when one talks to a native Christian of the upper ranks. There is then no great need for reserve save, of course, that the racial susceptibilities of the native gentleman who does not belong to the ruling class must be respected. Community of religion, in carrying the educated native Christian far away from the native Hindu or Muslim, brings him comparatively near to the European. Because he is a Christian he generally feels himself more in sympathy with his European rulers than he does with his fellow subjects of the same race and colour as himself.

Here I touch a matter of the utmost interest when one thinks of the more remote future of India. Political consequences greater than now appear may depend upon the spread of Christianity there, a spread whose progress, though at present scarcely perceptible in the upper classes, may possibly become much more rapid than it has been during the last century. I do not say that Hinduism or Islam is a cause of hostility to British rule. Neither do I suggest that a Christian native population would become fused with the European or Eurasian population. Colour might still operate against that, though hardly to such an extent as it does in keeping blacks and whites apart in North America. But if the number of Christians, especially in the middle and upper ranks of Indian society, were to increase, the difficulty of ascertaining native opinion, now so much felt by Indian administrators, would be perceptibly lessened, and the social separation of natives and Europeans might become less acute, to the great benefit of both sections of the population.

When we turn back to the Roman Empire how striking is the absence of any lines of religious demarcation! One must not speak of toleration as the note of its policy, because there was nothing to tolerate. All religions were equally true, or equally useful, each for its own country or nation. The satirist of an age which had already lost belief in the Olympian deities might scoff at the beast-gods of Egypt and the fanaticism which their worship evoked. But nobody thought of converting the devotees of crocodiles or cats. A Briton brought up by the Druids, or a Frisian who had worshipped Woden in his youth, found, if he was sent to command a garrison in Syria, no difficulty in attending a sacrifice to the Syrian Sun-god, or in marrying the daughter of the Sun-god's priest. Possibly the first injunctions to have regard to religion in choosing a consort that were ever issued in the ancient world were such as that given by St. Paul when he said, 'Be not unequally yoked together with unbelievers.' Christianity had a reason for this precept which the other religions had not, because to it all the other religions were false and pernicious, drawing men away from the only true God. We may accordingly say that, old-established and strong as some of the religions were which the Romans found when they began to conquer the Mediterranean countries, religion did not constitute an obstacle to the fusion of the peoples of those countries into one Roman nationality.

When the monotheistic religions came upon the scene, things began to change. Almost the only rebellions against Rome which were rather religious than political, were those of the Jews. When in the fourth, fifth, sixth, and seventh centuries, sharp theological controversies began to divide Christians, especially in the East, dangers appeared such as had never arisen from religious causes in the days of heathenism. Schisms, like that of the Donatists, and heresies, like that of the Montanists, began to trouble the field of politics. The Arian Goths and Vandals remained distinct from the orthodox provincials whom they conquered. In Egypt, a country always prone to fanaticism, the Monophysite antagonism to the Chalcedonian orthodoxy of the Eastern Emperors was so bitter that the native population showed signs of disaffection as early as the time of Justinian, and they offered, a century later, scarcely any resistance to those Musulman invaders from Arabia whom they disliked no more than they did their own sovereign at Constantinople.

A fourth agency working for fusion which the Roman Empire possessed, and which the English in India want, is to be found in language and literature. The conquests of Rome had been preceded by the spread of the Greek tongue and of Greek culture over the coasts of the Eastern Mediterranean. Even in the interior of Asia Minor and Syria, though the native languages continued to be spoken in the cities as late as the time of Tiberius [1], and probably held their ground in country districts down till the Arab conquest, Greek was understood by the richer people, and was a sort of *lingua franca* for commerce from Sicily to the Euphrates [2]. Greek literature was the basis of education, and formed the minds of the cultivated class. It was indeed familiar to that class even in the western half of the Empire, through which, by the time of the Antonines, Latin had begun to be generally spoken, except in remote regions

[1] As in Lycaonia; cf. Acts xiv.

[2] There is a curious story that when the head of Crassus was brought to the Parthian king a passage from the *Bacchae* of Euripides was recited by a Greek who was at the Court.

such as the Basque country and the banks of the Vaal and North-Western Gaul. As the process of unification usually works downwards from the wealthier and better educated to the masses, it was of the utmost consequence that the upper class should have, in these two great languages, a factor constantly operative in the assimilation of the ideas of peoples originally distinct, in the diffusion of knowledge, and in the creation of a common type of civilization. Just as the use of Latin and of the Vulgate maintained a sort of unity among Christian nations and races even in the darkest and most turbulent centuries of the Middle Ages, so the use of Latin and Greek throughout the whole Roman Empire powerfully tended to draw its parts together. Nor was it without importance that all the subjects of the Empire had the same models of poetic and prose style in the classical writers of Greece and in the Latin writers of the pre-Augustan and Augustan age. Virgil in particular became the national poet of the Empire, in whom imperial patriotism found its highest expression.

Very different have been the conditions of India. When the British came, they found no national literature, unless we can apply that name to the ancient Sanskrit epics, written in a tongue which had ceased to be spoken many centuries before. Persian and Arabic were cultivated languages, used by educated Musulmans and by a few Hindu servants of the Musulman princes. The *lingua franca* called Hindustani or Urdu, which had sprung up in the camps of the Mogul Emperors, was becoming a means of intercourse over Northern India, but was hardly used throughout the South. Only a handful of the population were sufficiently educated to be accessible to the influences of any literature, or spoke any tongue except that of their own district. At present five great languages [1], branches of the Aryan family,

[1] Hindi, Bengali, Marathi, Punjabi, and Gujarati.

divide between them Northern, North-Western, and Middle India, and four others[1] of the Dravidian type cover Southern India: while many others are spoken by smaller sections of the people. The language of the English conquerors, which was adopted as the official language in 1835, is the parent tongue of only about 250,000 persons out of 315,000,000, less than one in one thousand. An increasing number of natives of the educated class have learnt to speak it, and this number will continue to increase, but even if we reckon in these, it affects only an insignificant fraction of the population. I have already observed that it was an advantage for England in conquering India, and is an advantage for her in ruling it, that the inhabitants are so divided by language as well as by religion and (among the Hindus) by caste that they could not combine to resist her. Rome had enjoyed, in slighter measure, a similar advantage. But whereas in the Roman Empire Greek and Latin spread so swiftly and steadily that the various nationalities soon began to blend, the absence in India of any two such dominant tongues and the lower level of intellectual progress keep the vast bulk of the Indian population without any general vehicle for the interchange of thought or for the formation of any one type of literary and scientific culture. There is therefore no national literature for India, nor any prospect that one will arise. No Cicero forms prose style, no Virgil inspires an imperial patriotism. The English have established places of higher instruction on the model not so much of Oxford and Cambridge as of the Scottish or German Universities, and they have also created five examining Universities. Through these institutions they are giving to the ambitious youth of India, and especially to those who wish to enter Government employment or the learned professions, an education of a European type, a type

[1] Telugu, Tamil, Kanarese, Malayalam.

so remote from the natural quality and proclivities of the Indian mind that it is not likely to give birth to any literature with a distinctively Indian character. Indeed the chief effect of this instruction has so far been to make those who receive it cease to be Hindus or Musulmans without making them either Christians or Europeans. It acts as a powerful solvent, destroying the old systems of conventional morality, and putting little in their place. The results may not be seen for a generation or two. When they come they may prove far from happy.

If in the course of ages any one language comes to predominate in India and to be the language not only of commerce, law and administration, but also of literature, English is likely to be that language; and English will by that time have also become the leading language of the world[1]. This will tend both to unify the peoples of India and (in a sense) to bring them nearer to their rulers. By that time, however, if it ever arrives, so many other changes will also have arrived that it is vain to speculate on the type of civilization which will then have been produced.

These considerations have shown us how different have been the results of English from those of Roman conquest. In the latter case a double process began from the first. The provinces became assimilated to one another, and Rome became assimilated to them, or they to her. As her individuality passed to them it was diluted by their influence. Out of the one conquering race and the many conquered races there was growing up a people which, though many local distinctions remained, was by the end of the fourth century A. D. tending to become substantially one in religion, one in patriotism, one in its type of intellectual life and of material civilization.

[1] It is estimated that English is at present (1913) spoken by about 154 millions of persons, Russian by 100 millions, German by 80, Spanish by 60, French by 45. Of these English is increasing the most swiftly, Russian next, and then Spanish and German.

The process was never completed, because the end of the fourth century was just the time when the Empire began, not from any internal political discontents, but from financial and military weakness, and from religious dissensions which alienated the inhabitants of Egypt and Syria, to yield to invasions and immigrations which forced its parts asunder. But it was so far completed that Claudian could write in the days of Honorius: 'We who drink of the Rhone and the Orontes are all one nation.' In this one huge nation the city and people of Rome had been merged, their original character so obliterated that they could give their name to the world. But in India there has been neither a fusion of the conquerors and the conquered, nor even a fusion of the various conquered races into one people. Differences of race, language and religion have prevented the latter fusion; yet it may some day come. But a fusion of conquerors and conquered seems to be forbidden by climate and by the disparity of character and of civilization, as well as by antagonism of colour and religion. The English are too unlike the races of India, or any one of those races, to mingle with them, or to come to form, in the sense of Claudian's words, one people with them.

The nations and tribes that were overcome and incorporated by Rome were either, like the Greeks, the possessors of a civilization as old and as advanced as was her own, or else, like the Gauls and the Germans, belonged to stocks full of intellectual force, capable of receiving her lessons, and of rapidly rising to the level of her culture. The two greatest poets of the Augustan Age were a provincial peasant from Mantua, probably of Gallic stock, and the son of a freedman whose parents came from no one knows where. But the races of India were all of them far behind the English in material civilization. Some of them were and are intellectually backward;

others, whose keen intelligence and aptitude for learning equals that of Europeans, are inferior in energy and strength of will. Yet even these differences might not render an ultimate fusion impossible. It is religion and colour that seem to place that result beyond any horizon to which our eyes can reach. The semi-barbarous races of Southern and Western Siberia, comparatively few in numbers, will become Russians. The Georgians and Armenians of Transcaucasia, unless their attachment to their national churches saves them, may become Russians. Even the Turkmans of the Khanates will be Russians one day, as the Tatars of Kazan and the Crimea are already on the way to become. But the English seem destined to remain quite distinct from the natives of India, neither mingling their blood nor imparting their character and habits.

So too, it may be conjectured, there will not be, for ages to come, any fusion of North Americans with the races of the Philippine Isles, even if the United States continues to rule and to send its sons into that colonial dominion.

The observation that Rome effaced herself in giving her name and laws to the world suggests an inquiry into what may be called the retroactive influence of India upon England. In the annals of Rome, war conquest and territorial expansion pervade and govern the whole story. Her constitutional, her social, her economic history, from the end of the Samnite wars onwards, is substantially determined by her position as a ruling State, first in Italy and then in the Mediterranean world. It was the influence upon the City of the conditions which attached to her rule in the provinces that did most to destroy not only the old constitution but the old simple and upright character of the Roman people. The provinces avenged themselves upon their conquerors. In the end, Rome ceases to have any history of her own, except an architectural history, so completely is she merged in her Empire. To a great extent this is true of Italy as well as of Rome. Italy, which had subjected so many provinces, ends by becoming herself a province—a province no more important than the others, except in respect of the reverence that surrounded her name. Her history, from the time of Vespasian till that of Theodoric the Ostrogoth, is only a part of the history of the Empire. Quite otherwise with England. Though England has founded many colonies, sent out vast bodies of emigrants, and conquered wide dominions, her domestic history has been, since she lost Normandy and Aquitaine, comparatively little affected by these frequent wars and this immense expansion. One might compose a constitutional history of England, or an economic and industrial history, or an ecclesiastical history, or a literary history, or a social history, in which only few and slight references would need to be made to either the colonies or India. England was a great European power before she had any colonies or any Indian territories: and she would be a great European power if all of these transmarine possessions were to drop off. Only at a few moments in the century and a half since the battle of Plassy have Indian affairs gravely affected English politics. Every one remembers Fox's India Bill in 1783, and the trial of Warren Hastings, and the way in which the wealthy Nabobs seemed for a time to be demoralizing society and politics. It was in India that the Duke of Wellington first showed his military gifts. It was through the Indian opium trade that England first came into collision with China. The notion that Russian ambition might become dangerous to the security of Britain in India had something to do with the Crimean War, and with the subsequent policy towards the Turks followed by England down to 1880. The deplorable Afghan War of 1878-9 led, more perhaps than anything else, to the fall of Lord

Beaconsfield's Ministry in 1880. Other instances might be added in which Indian questions have told upon the foreign policy of Great Britain, or have given rise to parliamentary strife; although, by a tacit convention between the two great parties in England, efforts are usually made—and made most wisely—to prevent questions of Indian administration from becoming any further than seems absolutely necessary matters of party controversy. Yet, if all these instances be put together, they are less numerous and momentous than might have been expected when one considers the magnitude of the stake which Britain holds in India. And even when we add to these the effect of Indian markets upon British trade, and the undeniable influence of the possession of India upon the thoughts and aspirations of Englishmen, strengthening in them a sense of pride and what is called an imperial spirit, we shall still be surprised that the control of this vast territory and of a population more than seven times as large as that of the United Kingdom has not told more forcibly upon Britain, and coloured her history more deeply than it has in fact done.

Suppose that England had not conquered India. Would her domestic development, whether constitutional or social, have taken a course greatly different from that which it has actually followed? So far as we can judge, it would not. It has been the good fortune of England to stand far off from the conquered countries, and to have had a population too large to suffer sensibly from the moral evils which conquest and the influx of wealth bring in their train [1].

The remark was made at the outset of this discussion that the contact of the English race with native races in India, and the process by which the former is giving the material civilization, and a tincture of the intellec-

[1] The absence of slavery and the existence of Christianity will of course present themselves to every one's mind as other factors in differentiating the conditions of the modern from those of the Roman world.

tual culture, of Europe to a group of Asiatic peoples, is only part of that contact of European races with native races and of that Europeanizing of the latter by the former which is going on all over the world. France is doing a similar work in North Africa and Madagascar. Russia is doing it in Siberia and Turkistan and on the Amur. Germany is doing it in tropical Africa. England is doing it in Egypt and Borneo and Matabililand. The people of the United States are entering upon it in the Philippine Islands. Every one of these nations professes to be guided by philanthropic motives in its action. But it is not philanthropy that has carried any of them into these enterprises, nor is it clear that the immediate result will be to increase the sum of human happiness.

It is in India, however, that the process has been in progress for the longest time and on the largest scale. Even after a century's experience the results cannot be adequately judged, for the country is in a state of transition, with all sorts of new factors, such as railways and newspapers and colleges, working as well upon the humbler as upon the wealthier sections of the people. Three things, however, the career of the English in India has proved. One is, that it is possible for a European race to rule a subject native race on principles of strict justice, restraining the natural propensity of the stronger to abuse their power. India has been, and is, ruled upon such principles. When oppression or cruelty is perpetrated, it is not by the European official but by his native subordinates, and especially by the native police, whose delinquencies the European official cannot always discover. Scorn or insolence is sometimes displayed towards the natives by Europeans, and nothing does more to destroy the good effects of just government than such displays of scorn. But again, it is very seldom the European civil officials, but either private persons or occasionally junior officers in the army, who are guilty of this abuse of their racial superiority.

The second thing is that a relatively small body of European civilians, supported by a relatively small armed force, can maintain peace and order in an immense population standing on a lower plane of civilization, and itself divided by religious animosities bitter enough to cause the outbreak of intestine wars were the restraining hand withdrawn.

The third fact is that the existence of a system securing these benefits is compatible with an absolute separation between the rulers and the ruled. The chasm between them has in these hundred years of intercourse grown no narrower. Some even deem it wider, and regret the fact that the European official, who now visits England more easily and frequently, does not identify himself so thoroughly with India as did his predecessors some eighty years ago. As one of the greatest problems of this age, and of the age which will follow, is and must be the relation between the European races as a whole on the one hand, and the more backward races of a different colour on the other hand, this incompatibility of temper, this indisposition to be fused, or one may almost say, this impracticability of fusion, is a momentous result, full of significance for the future. It was quite otherwise with that first effort of humanity to draw itself together, which took shape in the fusion of the races that Rome conquered, and the creation of one Græco-Roman type of civilization for them. But the conditions of that small ancient world were very different from those by which mankind finds itself now confronted.

It is impossible to think of the future and to recall that first impulse towards the unity of mankind which closed fourteen centuries ago, without reverting once more to the Roman Empire, and asking whether the events which caused, and the circumstances which accompanied, its dissolution throw any light on the probable fate of British dominion in the East.

Empires die sometimes by violence and sometimes by disease. Frequently they die from a combination of the two, that is to say, some wasting disease so reduces their vitality that a small amount of external violence suffices to extinguish the feeble life. It was so with the dominion of Rome. To outward appearance it was the irruption of the barbarians from the north that tore away the provinces in the West, as it was the assaults of the Turks ending with the capture of Constantinople in 1453 that gave the last death blow to the weakened and narrowed Empire which still lingered on in the East. But the dissolution and dismemberment of the western Roman Empire, beginning with the abandonment of Britain in A. D. 411, and ending with the establishment of the Lombards in Italy in A. D. 568, with the conquest of Africa by the Arab chief Sidi Okba in the seventh century, and with the capture of Sicily by Musulman fleets in the ninth, were really due to internal causes which had been for a long time at work. In some provinces at least the administration had become inefficient or corrupt, and the humbler classes were oppressed by the more powerful. The population had in many regions been diminished, and in nearly all it had become unwarlike, so that barbarian levies, raised on the frontier, had taken the place of native troops. The revenue was unequal to the task of maintaining an army sufficient for defence. How far the financial straits to which the government was reduced were due to the exhaustion of the soil, how far to maladministration is not altogether easy to determine. They had doubtless been aggravated by the disorders and invasions of A. D. 260-282. Neither can we tell whether the intellectual capacity of the ruling class and the physical vigour of the bulk of the population may not have declined. But it seems pretty clear that the armies and the revenue that were at the disposal of Trajan would have been sufficient to defend the Empire three centuries later, when the first fatal blows were struck; and we may therefore say that it was really from internal maladies, from anaemia or atrophy, from the want of men and the want of money, perhaps also from the want of wisdom, rather than from the appearance of more formidable foes, that the Roman dominion perished in the West.

British power in India shows no similar signs of weakness, for though the establishment of internal peace is beginning to make it less easy to recruit the native army with first-class fighting-men, such as the Punjab used to furnish, it has been hitherto found possible to keep that army up to its old standard of numbers and efficiency. Still the warning Rome has bequeathed is a warning not to be neglected. Her great difficulty was finance and the impoverishment of the cultivator. Finance and the poverty of the cultivator, who is still, though much less than formerly, in danger of famine, and is taxed to the full measure of his capacity—these are the standing difficulties of Indian administration; and they do not grow less, for, as population increases, the struggle for food is more severe, and the expenditure on frontier defence, including strategic railways, has gone on rapidly increasing. Fortunately the extension of tillage by the improvement of irrigation facilities, and the greatly increased capacity of the railway system to bring food into districts which may be at any moment suffering from drought, has reduced the dangers of famine. There is still some suffering and an increased death rate in such districts, but there is now hardly any starvation.

As England seems to be quite as safe from rebellion within India as was Rome within her Empire, so is she stronger against external foes than Rome was, for she has far more defensible frontiers, viz. the sea which she commands, and a tremendous mountain barrier in whose barren gorges a comparatively small force might repel invaders coming from a distance and obliged to carry their food with them. There is really, so far as can be seen at present, only one danger against which the English have to guard, that of provoking discontent among their subjects by laying on them too heavy a burden of taxation. It has been suggested that when the differences of caste and religion which now separate the peoples of India from one another have begun to disappear, when European civilization has drawn them together into one people, and European ideas have created a large class of educated and restless natives ill disposed to brook subjection to an alien race, new dangers may arise to threaten the permanence of British power. Such possibilities, however, belong to a future which seems still distant.

It is, of course, upon England in the last resort that the defence of India rests. The task is well within her strength, though serious enough to make it fitting that a prudent and pacific spirit should guide her whole foreign and colonial policy, that she should neither embark on needless wars nor lay on herself the burden of holding down disaffected subjects.

England must be prepared to command the sea, and to spare eighty thousand of her soldiers to garrison the country. Were she ever to find herself unable to do this, what would become of India? Its political unity, which depends entirely on the English Raj, would vanish like a morning mist. Wars would break out, wars of ambition, or plunder, or religion, which might end in the ascendency of a few adventurers, not necessarily belonging to the reigning native dynasties, but probably either Pathans, or Sikhs, or Musulmans of the north-west. The Marathas might rise in the West. The Nepalese might descend upon Bengal. Or perhaps the country would, after an interval of chaos, pass into the hands of some other European Power. To India severance from England would mean confusion, bloodshed, and pillage. To England however, apart from the particular events which might have caused the snapping of the tie, and apart from the possible loss of a market, severance from India need involve no lasting injury. To be mistress of a vast country whose resources for defence need to be supplemented by her own, adds indeed to her fame, but does not add to her strength. England was great and powerful before she owned a yard of land in Asia, and might be great and powerful again with no more foothold in the East than would be needed for the naval fortresses which protect her commerce.

Happily for England and for India, questions such as these are for the moment purely speculative.

II

THE EXTENSION OF ROMAN AND ENGLISH LAW THROUGHOUT THE WORLD

I. The Regions covered by Roman and English Law.

From the general comparison contained in the preceding Essay of Rome and England as powers conquering and administering territories beyond their original limits, it is natural to pass on to consider one particular department of the work which territorial extension has led them to undertake, viz. their action as makers of a law which has spread far out over the world. Both nations have built up legal systems which are now—for the Roman law has survived the Roman Empire, and is full of vitality to-day—in force over immense areas that were unknown to those who laid the foundations of both systems. In this respect Rome and England stand alone among nations, unless we reckon in the law of Islam which, being a part of the religion of Islam, governs Musulmans wherever Musulmans are to be found.

Roman law, more or less modified by national or local family customs or land customs and by modern legislation, prevails to-day in all the European countries which formed part either of the ancient or of the mediaeval Roman Empire, that is to say, in Italy, in Greece and the rest of South-Eastern Europe (so far as the Christian part of the population is concerned), in Spain, Portugal, Switzerland, France, Germany (including the German and Slavonic parts of the Austro-Hungarian monarchy), Belgium, Holland. The only exception is South Britain, which lost its Roman law with the coming of the Angles and Saxons in the fifth century. The leading principles of Roman jurisprudence prevail also in some other outlying countries which have borrowed much of their law from some one or more of the countries already named, viz. Denmark, Norway, Sweden, Russia, and Hungary. Then come the non-European colonies settled by some among the above-named nations, such as Louisiana, the Canadian province of Quebec, Ceylon, British Guiana, South Africa (all the above having been at one time colonies either of France or of Holland), German Africa, and French Africa, together with the regions which formerly obeyed Spain or Portugal, including Mexico, Central America, South America, Cuba, and the Philippine Islands. Add to these the Dutch and French East Indies, and Siberia. There is also Scotland, which has, since the establishment of the Court of Session by King James the Fifth in 1532, built up its law out of Roman Civil and (to some slight extent) Roman Canon Law [1].

English law is in force not only in England, Wales, and Ireland but also in most of the British colonies. Quebec, Ceylon, Mauritius, South Africa, and some few of the West Indian islands follow the Roman law [2]. The rest, including Australia, New Zealand, and all Canada except Quebec, follow English; as does also the United

[1] There is scarcely a trace of Celtic custom in modern Scottish law. The law of land, however, is largely of feudal origin; and commercial law has latterly been influenced by that of England.

[2] In these British West Indian islands, however, that which remains of Spanish law, as in Trinidad and Tobago, and of French law, as in St. Vincent, is now comparatively slight; and before long the West Indies (except Cuba and Puerto Rico, Guadeloupe and Martinique) will be entirely under English law. See as to the British colonies generally, Sir C. P. Ilbert's *Legislative Methods and Forms*, chap. ix.

States, except Louisiana, but with the Hawaiian Islands, and India, though in India, as we shall see, native law is also administered.

Thus between them these two systems cover nearly the whole of the civilized, and most of the uncivilized world. Only two considerable masses of population stand outside—the Musulman East, that is, Turkey, North Africa, Persia, Western Turkistan and Afghanistan, which obey the sacred law of Islam, and China, which has customs all her own. It is hard to estimate the total number of human beings who live under the English common law, for one does not know whether to reckon in the semi-savage natives of such regions as Uganda, for instance, or Fiji. But there are probably one hundred and forty millions of civilized persons (without counting the natives of India) who do: and the number living under some modern form of the Roman law is still larger.

It is of the process by which two systems which had their origin in two small communities, the one an Italian city, the other a group of Teutonic tribes, have become extended over nine-tenths of the globe that I propose to speak in the pages that follow. There are analogies between the forms which the process took in the two cases. There are also contrasts. The main contrast is that whereas we may say that (roughly speaking) Rome extended her law by conquest, that is, by the spreading of her military power, England has extended hers by settlement, that is, by the spreading out of her race. In India, however, conquest rather than colonization has been the agency employed by England, and it is therefore between the extension of English law to India and the extension of Roman law to the Roman Empire that the best parallel can be drawn. It need hardly be added that the Roman law has been far more changed in descending to the modern world and becoming adapted to modern conditions of life than the law of England has been in its extension over new areas. That extension is an affair of the last three centuries only, and the whole history of English law is of only some eleven centuries, reckoning from the West Saxon kings Ine and Alfred, let us say, to A. D. 1900, or of eight, if we begin with King Henry the Second, whereas that of Roman law covers twenty-five centuries, of which all but the first three have witnessed the process of extension, so early did Rome begin to impose her law upon her subjects. To the changes, however, which have passed on the substance of the law we shall return presently. Let us begin by examining the causes and circumstances which induced the extension to the whole ancient world of rules and doctrines that had grown up in a small city.

II. The Diffusion of Roman Law by Conquest

The first conquests of Rome were made in Italy. They did not, however, involve any legal changes, for conquest meant merely the reduction of what had been an independent city or group of cities or tribes to vassalage, with the obligation of sending troops to serve in the Roman armies. Local autonomy was not (as a rule) interfered with; and such autonomy included civil jurisdiction, so the Italic and Græco-Italic cities continued to be governed by their own laws, which (in the case at least of Oscan and Umbrian communities) usually resembled that of Rome, and which of course tended to become assimilated to it even before Roman citizenship was extended to the Italian allies. With the annexation of part of Sicily in A. D. 230 the first provincial government was set up, and the legal and administrative problems which Rome had to deal with began to show themselves. Other provinces were added in pretty rapid succession, the last being Britain (invaded under Claudius in A. D. 43). Now although in all these provinces the Romans had to maintain order, to collect revenue and to dispense justice, the conditions under which these things, and especially the dispensing of justice, had to be done differed much in different provinces. Some, such as Sicily, Achaia, Macedonia and the provinces of Western Asia Minor, as well as Africa (*i. e.* such parts of that province as Carthage had permeated), were civilized countries, where law-courts already existed in the cities [1]. The laws had doubtless almost everywhere been created by custom, for the so-called Codes we hear of in Greek cities were often rather in the nature of political constitutions and penal enactments than summarized statements of the whole private law; yet in some cities the customs had been so summarized [2]. Other provinces, such as those of Thrace, Transalpine Gaul, Spain, and Britain, were in a lower stage of social organization, and possessed, when they were conquered, not so much regular laws as tribal usages, suited to their rude inhabitants. In the former set of cases not much new law was needed. In the latter set the native customs could not meet the needs of communities which soon began to advance in wealth and culture under Roman rule, so law had to be created.

There were also in all these provinces two classes of inhabitants. One consisted of those who enjoyed Roman citizenship, not merely men of Italian birth settled there but also men to whom citizenship had been granted (as for instance when they retired from military service), or the natives of cities on which (as in the case of Tarsus, St. Paul's birthplace) citizenship had been conferred as a

[1] Cicero says of Sicily, 'Siculi hoc iure sunt ut quod civis cum cive agat, domi certet suis legibus; quod Siculus cum Siculo non eiusdem civitatis, ut de eo praetor iudices sortiatur'; *In Verrem*, ii. 13, 32.

[2] The laws of Gortyn in Crete, recently published from an inscription discovered there, apparently of about 500 B. C., are a remarkable instance. Though not a complete code, they cover large parts of the field of law.

boon[1]. This was a large class, and went on rapidly increasing. To it pure Roman law was applicable, subject of course to any local customs.

The other class consisted of the provincial subjects who were merely subjects, and, in the view of the Roman law, aliens (*peregrini*). They had their own laws or tribal customs, and to them Roman law was primarily inapplicable, not only because it was novel and unfamiliar, so strange to their habits that it would have been unjust as well as practically inconvenient to have applied it to them, but also because the Romans, like the other civilized communities of antiquity, had been so much accustomed to consider private legal rights as necessarily connected with membership of a city community that it would have seemed unnatural to apply the private law of one city community to the citizens of another. It is true that the Romans after a time disabused their minds of this notion, as indeed they had from a comparatively early period extended their own private civil rights to many of the cities which had become their subject allies. Still it continued to influence them at the time (B. C. 230 to 120) when they were laying out the lines of their legal policy for the provinces.

Of that legal policy I must speak quite briefly, partly because our knowledge, though it has been enlarged of late years by the discovery and collection of a great mass of inscriptions, is still imperfect, partly because I could not set forth the details without going into a number of technical points which might perplex readers unacquainted with the Roman law. It is only the main

[1] When I speak of citizenship, it is not necessarily or generally political citizenship that is to be understood, but the citizenship which carried with it private civil rights (those rights which the Romans call *connubium* and *commercium*), including Roman family and inheritance law and Roman contract and property law. Not only the civilized Spaniards but the bulk of the upper class in Greece seem to have become citizens by the time of the Antonines.

lines on which the conquerors proceeded that can be here indicated.

Every province was administered by a governor with a staff of subordinate officials, the higher ones Roman, and (under the Republic) remaining in office only so long as did the governor. The governor was the head of the judicial as well as the military and civil administration, just as the consuls at Rome originally possessed judicial as well as military and civil powers, and just as the praetor at Rome, though usually occupied with judicial work, had also both military and civil authority. The governor's court was the proper tribunal for those persons who in the provinces enjoyed Roman citizenship, and in it Roman law was applied to such persons in matters touching their family relations, their rights of inheritance, their contractual relations with one another, just as English law is applied to Englishmen in Cyprus or Hong Kong. No special law was needed for them. As regards the provincials, they lived under their own law, whatever it might be, subject to one important modification. Every governor when he entered his province issued an Edict setting forth certain rules which he proposed to apply during his term of office. These rules were to be valid only during his term, for his successor issued a fresh Edict, but in all probability each reproduced nearly all of what the preceding Edict had contained. Thus the same general rules remained continuously in force, though they might be modified in detail, improvements which experience had shown to be necessary being from time to time introduced[1]. This was the method which the praetors followed at Rome, so the provincial governors had a precedent for it and knew how to work it. Now the Edict seems to have contained, besides its provisions regarding the collection

[1] As to this see Essay XIV in the author's *Studies in History and Jurisprudence*.

of revenue and civil administration in general, certain more specifically legal regulations, intended to indicate the action which the governor's court would take not only in disputes arising between Roman citizens, but also in those between citizens and aliens, and probably also to some extent in those between aliens themselves. Where the provisions of the Edict did not apply, aliens would be governed by their own law. In cities municipally organized, and especially in the more civilized provinces, the local city courts would doubtless continue to administer, as they had done before the Romans came, their local civil law; and in the so-called free cities, which had come into the Empire as allies, these local courts had for a long time a wide scope for their action. Criminal law, however, would seem to have fallen within the governor's jurisdiction, at any rate in most places and for the graver offences, because criminal law is the indispensable guarantee for public order and for the repression of sedition or conspiracy, matters for which the governor was of course responsible [1]. Thus the governor's court was not only that which dispensed justice between Roman citizens, and which dealt with questions of revenue, but was also the tribunal for cases between citizens and aliens, and for the graver criminal proceedings. It was apparently also a court which entertained some kinds of suits between aliens, as for instance between aliens belonging to different cities, or in districts where no regular municipal courts existed, and (probably) dealt with appeals from those courts where they did exist. Moreover where aliens even of the same city chose to resort to it they could apparently do so. I speak of courts rather than of law, because it must be remembered that although we are naturally inclined to think of law as coming first, and courts being afterwards

[1] In St. Paul's time, however, the venerable Athenian Areopagus may have retained a certain jurisdiction; cf. Acts xvii, 19. The Romans treated Athens with special consideration.

created to administer law, it is really courts that come first, and that by their action build up law partly out of customs observed by the people and partly out of their own notions of justice. This, which is generally true of all countries, is of course specially true of countries where law is still imperfectly developed, and of places where different classes of persons, not governed by the same legal rules, have to be dealt with.

The Romans brought some experience to the task of creating a judicial administration in the provinces, where both citizens and aliens had to be considered, for Rome herself had become, before she began to acquire territories outside Italy, a place of residence or resort for alien traders, so that as early as B. C. 247 she created a magistrate whose special function it became to handle suits between aliens, or in which one party was an alien. This magistrate built up, on the basis of mercantile usage, equity, and common sense, a body of rules fit to be applied between persons whose native law was not the same; and the method he followed would naturally form a precedent for the courts of the provincial governors.

Doubtless the chief aim, as well as the recognized duty, of the governors was to disturb provincial usage as little as they well could. The temptations to which they were exposed, and to which they often succumbed, did not lie in the direction of revolutionizing local law in order to introduce either purely Roman doctrines or any artificial uniformity [1]. They would have made trouble for themselves had they attempted this. And why should they attempt it? The ambitious governors desired military fame. The bad ones wanted money. The better men, such as Cicero, and in later days the younger Pliny, liked to be fêted by the provincials and have

[1] One of the charges against Verres was that he disregarded all kinds of law alike. Under him, says Cicero, the Sicilians 'neque suas leges neque nostra senatus consulta neque communia iura tenuerunt'; *In Verr.* i. 4, 13.

statues erected to them by grateful cities. No one of these objects was to be attained by introducing legal reforms which theory might suggest to a philosophic statesman, but which nobody asked for. It seems safe to assume from what we know of official human nature elsewhere, that the Roman officials took the line of least resistance compatible with the raising of money and the maintenance of order. These things being secured, they would be content to let other things alone.

Things, however, have a way of moving even when officials may wish to let them rest. When a new and vigorous influence is brought into a mixture of races receptive rather than resistent (as happened in Asia Minor under the Romans), or when a higher culture acts through government upon a people less advanced but not less naturally gifted (as happened in Gaul under the Romans), changes must follow in law as well as in other departments of human action. Here two forces were at work. One was the increasing number of persons who were Roman citizens, and therefore lived by the Roman law. The other was the increasing tendency of the government to pervade and direct the whole public life of the province. When monarchy became established as the settled form of the Roman government, provincial administration began to be better organized, and a regular body of bureaucratic officials presently grew up. The jurisdiction of the governor's court extended itself, and was supplemented in course of time by lower courts administering law according to the same rules. The law applied to disputes arising between citizens and noncitizens became more copious and definite. The provincial Edicts expanded and became well settled as respects the larger part of their contents. So by degrees the law of the provinces was imperceptibly Romanized in its general spirit and leading conceptions, probably also in such particular departments as the original local law of the particular province had not fully covered. But the process did not proceed at the same rate in all the provinces, nor did it result in a uniform legal product, for a good deal of local customary law remained, and this customary law of course differed in different provinces. In the Hellenic and Hellenized countries the pre-existing law was naturally fuller and stronger than in the West; and it held its ground more effectively than the ruder usages of Gauls or Spaniards, obtaining moreover a greater respect from the Romans, who felt their intellectual debt to the Greeks.

It may be asked what direct legislation there was during this period for the provinces. Did the Roman *Comitia* (popular Assembly) either pass statutes for them, as the British Parliament has sometimes done for India, or did the *Comitia* establish in each province some legislative authority? So far as private law went Rome did neither during the republican period[1]. The necessity was not felt, because any alterations made in Roman law proper altered it for Roman citizens who dwelt in the provinces no less than for those in Italy, while as to provincial aliens, the Edict of the governor and the rules which the practice of his courts established were sufficient to introduce any needed changes. But the Senate issued decrees intended to operate in the provinces, and when the Emperors began to send instructions to their provincial governors or to issue declarations of their will in any other form, these had the force of law, and constituted a body of legislation, part of which was general, while part was special to the province for which it was issued.

Meantime—and I am now speaking particularly of the three decisively formative centuries from B. C. 150 to A. D. 150—another process had been going on even

[1] The *Lex Sempronia* mentioned by Livy, xxxv. 7, seems to be an exception, due to very special circumstances.

more important. The Roman law itself had been changing its character, had been developing from a rigid and highly technical system, archaic in its forms and harsh in its rules, preferring the letter to the spirit, and insisting on the strict observance of set phrases, into a liberal and elastic system, pervaded by the principles of equity and serving the practical convenience of a cultivated and commercial community [1]. Its result was to permeate the original law of Rome applicable to citizens only (*ius civile*) with the law which had been constructed for the sake of dealing with aliens (*ius gentium*), so that the product was a body of rules fit to be used by any civilized people, as being grounded in reason and utility, while at the same time both copious in quantity and refined in quality.

This result had been reached about A. D. 150, by which time the laws of the several provinces had also been largely Romanized. Thus each body of law—if we may venture for this purpose to speak of provincial law as a whole—had been drawing nearer to the other. The old law of the city of Rome had been expanded and improved till it was fit to be applied to the provinces. The various laws of the various provinces had been constantly absorbing the law of the city in the enlarged and improved form latterly given to it. Thus when at last the time for a complete fusion arrived the differences between the two had been so much reduced that the fusion took place easily and naturally, with comparatively little disturbance of the state of things already in existence. The traveller sometimes finds on the southern side of the Alps two streams running in neighbouring valleys. One which has issued from a glacier slowly deposits as it flows over a rocky bed the white mud which it brought from its icy cradle. The other which rose from

[1] The nature of this process is described in the author's *Studies in History and Jurisprudence*. See especially Essay XI and Essay XIV.

clear springs gradually gathers colouring matter as in its lower course it cuts through softer strata or through alluvium. When at last they meet, the glacier torrent has become so nearly clear that the tint of its waters is scarcely distinguishable from that of the originally bright but now slightly turbid affluent. Thus Roman and provincial law, starting from different points but pursuing a course in which their diversities were constantly reduced, would seem to have become so similar by the end of the second century A. D. that there were few marked divergences, so far as private civil rights and remedies were concerned, between the position of citizens and that of aliens.

Here, however, let a difference be noted. The power of assimilation was more complete in some branches of law than it was in others; and it was least complete in matters where old standing features of national character and feeling were present. In the Law of Property and Contract it had advanced so far as to have become, with some few exceptions [1], substantially identical. The same may be said of Penal Law and the system of legal procedure. But in the Law of Family Relations and in that of Inheritance, a matter closely connected with family relations, the dissimilarities were still significant; and we shall find this phenomenon reappearing in the history of English and Native Law in India.

Two influences which I have not yet dwelt upon had been, during the second century, furthering the assimilation. One was the direct legislation of the Emperor which, scanty during the first age of the monarchy, had now become more copious, and most of which was intended to operate upon citizens and aliens alike. The other was the action of the Emperor as supreme judicial

[1] Such as the technical peculiarities of the Roman *stipulatio*, and those of the Greek *syngraphe*.

authority, sometimes in matters brought directly before him for decision, more frequently as judge of appeals from inferior tribunals. He had a council called the Consistory which acted on his behalf, because, especially in the troublous times which began after the reign of Marcus Aurelius and presaged the ultimate dissolution of the Empire, the sovereign was seldom able to preside in person. The judgments of the Consistory, being delivered in the Emperor's name on his behalf, and having equal authority with statutes issued by him, must have done much to make law uniform in all the provinces and among all classes of subjects [1].

III. The Establishment of One Law for the Empire.

Finally, in the beginning of the third century A. D., the decisive step was taken. The distinction between citizens and aliens vanished by the grant of full citizenship to all subjects of the Empire, a grant however which may have been, in the first instance, applied only to organized communities, and not also to the backward sections of the rural population, in Corsica, for instance, or in some of the Alpine valleys. Our information as to the era to which this famous Edict of Antoninus Caracalla belongs is lamentably scanty. Gaius, who is the best authority for the middle period of the law, lived fifty or sixty years earlier. The compilers of Justinian's *Digest*, which is the chief source of our knowledge for the law as a whole, lived three hundred years later, when the old distinctions between the legal rights of citizens and those of aliens had become mere matters of antiquarian curiosity. These

[1] These *decreta* of the Emperor were reckoned among his *Constitutiones* (as to which see *Studies in History and Jurisprudence*, Essay XIV). There does not seem to have been any public record kept and published of them, but many of them would doubtless become diffused through the law schools and otherwise. The first regular collections of imperial constitutions known to us belong to a later time.

compilers therefore modified the passages of the older jurists which they inserted in the *Digest* so as to make them suit their own more recent time. As practical men they were right, but they have lessened the historical value of these fragments of the older jurists, just as the modern restorer of a church spoils it for the purposes of architectural history, when he alters it to suit his own ideas of beauty or convenience. Still it may fairly be assumed that when Caracalla's grant of citizenship was made the bulk of the people, or at least of the town dwellers, had already obtained either a complete or an incomplete citizenship in the more advanced provinces, and that those who had not were at any rate enjoying under the provincial Edicts most of the civil rights that had previously been confined to citizens, such for instance as the use of the so-called Praetorian Will with its seven seals.

How far the pre-existing local law of different provinces or districts was superseded at one stroke by this extension of citizenship, or in other words, what direct and immediate change was effected in the modes of jurisdiction and in the personal relations of private persons, is a question which we have not the means of answering. Apparently many difficulties arose which further legislation, not always consistent, was required to deal with [1]. One would naturally suppose that where Roman rules differed materially from those which a provincial community had followed, the latter could not have been suddenly substituted for the former.

A point, for instance, about which we should like to be better informed is whether the Roman rules which gave to the father his wide power over his children and their children were forthwith extended to provincial families. The Romans themselves looked upon this paternal power as an institution peculiar to themselves.

[1] See upon this subject the learned and acute treatise (by which I have been much aided) of Dr. L. Mitteis, *Reichsrecht und Volksrecht in den östlichen Provinzen des Römischen Kaiserreichs,* Chap. VI.

To us moderns, and especially to Englishmen and Americans, it seems so oppressive that we cannot but suppose it was different in practice from what it looks on paper. And although it had lost some of its old severity by the time of the Antonines, one would think that communities which had not grown up under it could hardly receive it with pleasure.

From the time of Caracalla (A. D. 211-217) down till the death of Theodosius the Great (A. D. 395) the Empire had, broadly speaking, only one law. There was, however, a certain amount of special legislation for particular provinces, and a good deal of customary law peculiar to certain provinces or parts of them. Although before the time of Justinian it would seem that every Roman subject, except the half-barbarous peoples on the frontiers, such as the Soanes and Abkhasians of the Caucasus or the Ethiopic tribes of Nubia, and except a very small class of freedmen placed under special disabilities, was in the enjoyment of Roman citizenship, with private rights substantially the same, yet it is clear that in the East some Roman principles and maxims were never fully comprehended by the mass of the inhabitants and their legal advisers of the humbler sort, while other principles did not succeed in altogether displacing the rules to which the people were attached. We have evidence in recently recovered fragments of an apparently widely used law-book, Syriac and Armenian copies of which remain, that this was the case in the Eastern provinces, and no doubt it was so in others also. In Egypt, for instance, it may be gathered from the fragments of papyri which are now being published, that the old native customs, overlaid or re-moulded to some extent by Greek law, held their ground even down to the sixth or seventh century [1].

[1] This is carefully worked out both as to Syria and to Egypt by Dr. Mitteis, *op. cit.* He thinks (pp. 30-33) that the law of the Syrian book, where it departs from pure Roman law as we find it in the *Corpus Iuris*, is mainly of Greek origin, though with traces of Eastern custom. He also suggests that

Still, after making all allowance for these provincial variations, philosophic jurisprudence and a levelling despotism had done their work, and given to the civilized world, for the first and last time in its history, one harmonious body of legal rules.

The causes which enabled the Romans to achieve this result were, broadly speaking, the five following:—

(1) There was no pre-existing body of law deeply rooted and strong enough to offer resistance to the spread of Roman law. Where any highly developed system of written rules or customs existed, it existed only in cities, such as those of the Greek or Graecized provinces on both sides of the Aegean. The large countries, Pontus, for instance, or Thrace or Gaul, were in a legal sense unorganized or backward. Thus the Romans had, if not a blank sheet to write on, yet no great difficulty in overspreading or dealing freely with what they found.

(2) There were no forms of faith which had so interlaced religious feelings and traditions with the legal notions and customs of the people as to give those notions and customs a tenacious grip on men's affection. Except among the Jews, and to some extent among the Egyptians, Rome had no religious force to overcome such as Islam and Hinduism present in India.

(3) The grant of Roman citizenship to a community or an individual was a privilege highly valued, because it meant a rise in social status and protection against arbitrary treatment by officials. Hence even those who might have liked their own law better were glad to part with it for the sake of the immunities of a Roman citizen.

(4) The Roman governor and the Roman officials in general had an administrative discretion wider than

the opposition, undoubtedly strong, of the Eastern Monophysites to the Orthodox Emperors at Constantinople may have contributed to make the Easterners cling the closer to their own customary law. The Syrian book belongs to the fifth century A. D., and is therefore earlier than Justinian (Bruns und Sachau, *Syrisch-römisches Rechtsbuch aus dem fünften Jahrhundert*).

officials enjoy under most modern governments, and certainly wider than either a British or an United States legislature would delegate to any person. Hence Roman governors could by their Edicts and their judicial action mould the law and give it a shape suitable to the needs of their province with a freedom of handling which facilitated the passage from local law or custom to the jurisprudence of the Empire generally.

(5) Roman law itself, *i. e.* the law of the City, went on expanding and changing, ridding itself of its purely national and technical peculiarities, till it became fit to be the law of the whole world. This process kept step with, and was the natural expression of, the political and social assimilation of Rome to the provinces and of the provinces to Rome.

At the death of Theodosius the Great the Roman Empire was finally divided into an Eastern and a Western half; so that thenceforward there were two legislative authorities. For the sake of keeping the law as uniform as possible, arrangements were made for the transmission by each Emperor to the other of such ordinances as he might issue, in order that these might be, if approved, issued for the other half of the Empire. These arrangements, however, were not fully carried out: and before long the Western Empire drifted into so rough a sea that legislation practically stopped. The great Codex of Theodosius the Second (a collection of imperial enactments published in A. D. 438) was however promulgated in the Western as well as in the Eastern part of the Empire, whereas the later Codex and Digest of Justinian, published nearly a century later, was enacted only for the East, though presently extended (by the re-conquest in Justinian's reign) to Italy, Sicily, and Africa. Parts of the Theodosian Codex were embodied in the manuals of law made for the use of their Roman subjects by some of the barbarian kings. It continued to be recognized in the Western provinces after the extinction of the imperial line in the West in A. D. 476: and was indeed, along with the manuals aforesaid, the principal source whence during a long period the Roman population drew their law in the provinces out of which the kingdoms of the Franks, Burgundians, and Visigoths were formed.

Then came the torpor of the Dark Ages.

IV. The Extension of Roman Law after the Fall of the Western Empire.

Upon the later history of the Roman law and its diffusion through the modern world I can but briefly touch, for I should be led far away from the special topic here considered. The process of extension went on in some slight measure by conquest, but mainly by peaceful means, the less advanced peoples, who had no regular legal system of their own, being gradually influenced by and learning from their more civilized neighbours to whom the Roman system had descended. The light of legal knowledge radiated forth from two centres, from Constantinople over the Balkanic and Euxine countries between the tenth and the fifteenth centuries, from Italy over the lands that lay north and west of her from the twelfth to the sixteenth century. Thereafter it is Germany, Holland, and France that have chiefly propagated the imperial law, Germany by her universities and writers, France and Holland both through their jurists and as colonizing powers.

In the history of the mediaeval and modern part of the process of extension five points or stages of especial import may be noted.

The first is the revival of legal study which began in Italy towards the end of the eleventh century A. D., and the principal agent in which was the school of Bologna, famous for many generations thereafter. From that date onward the books of Justinian, which had before that time been superseded in the Eastern Empire by later legislation, were lectured and commented on in the universities of Italy, France, Spain, England, Germany, and have continued to be so till our own day. They formed, except in England where from the time of Henry the Third onwards they had a powerful and at last a victorious rival in the Common Law, the basis of all legal training and knowledge.

The second is the creation of that vast mass of rules for the guidance of ecclesiastical matters and courts—courts whose jurisdiction was in the Middle Ages far wider than it is now—which we call the Canon Law. These rules, drawn from the canons of Councils and decrees of Popes, began to be systematized during the twelfth century, and were first consolidated into an ordered body by Pope Gregory the Ninth in the middle of the thirteenth [1]. They were so largely based on the Roman law that we may describe them as being substantially a development of it, partly on a new side, partly in a new spirit, and though they competed with the civil law of the temporal courts, they also extended the intellectual and moral influence of that law.

The third is the acceptance of the Roman law as being of binding authority in countries which had not previously owned it, and particularly in Germany and Scotland. It was received in Germany because the German king (after the time of Otto the Great) was deemed to be also Roman Emperor, the legitimate successor of the far-off assemblies and magistrates and Emperors of old Rome; and its diffusion was aided by the fact that German lawyers had mostly received their legal training at Italian universities. It came in gradually as subsidiary to Germanic customs, but the judges, trained in Italy in

[1] Other parts were added later.

the Roman system, required the customs to be proved, and so by degrees Roman doctrines supplanted them, though less in the Saxon districts, where a native law-book, the *Sachsenspiegel,* had already established its influence. The acceptance nowhere went so far as to supersede the whole customary law of Germany, whose land-rights, for instance, retained their feudal character. The formal declaration of the general validity of the *Corpus Iuris* in Germany is usually assigned to the foundation by the Emperor Maximilian I, in 1495, of the Imperial Court of Justice (*Reichskammergericht*). As Holland was then still a part of the Germanic Empire, as well as of the Burgundian heritage which had passed to Maximilian, it was the law of Holland also, and so has become the law of Java, of Celebes, of Ceylon, and of South Africa. In Scotland it was adopted at the foundation of the Court of Session, on the model of the Parlement of Paris, by King James the Fifth. Political antagonism to England and political attraction to France, together with the influence of the Canonists, naturally determined the King and the Court to follow the system which prevailed on the European continent.

The fourth stage is that of codification. In many parts of Roman Gaul as it passed into feudal France, though less in Provence and Languedoc than elsewhere, the Roman law had gone back into that shape of a body of customs from which it had emerged a thousand years before; and in Northern and Middle France some customs, especially in matters relating to land, were not Roman at all. At last, under Lewis the Fourteenth, a codifying process set in. Comprehensive Ordinances, each covering a branch of law, began to be issued from 1667 down to 1747. These operated throughout France, and, being founded on Roman principles, further advanced the work, already prosecuted by the jurists, of Romanizing the customary law of Northern France.

That of Southern France (the *pays du droit écrit*) had been more specially Roman, for the South had been less affected by Frankish conquest and settlement. The five Codes promulgated by Napoleon followed in 1803 to 1810[1]. Others reproducing them with more or less divergence have been enacted in other countries speaking Romance languages.

In Prussia, King Frederick the Second directed the preparation of a Code which became law after his death, in 1794. From 1848 onwards parts of the law of Germany (which differed in different parts of the country) began to be codified, being at first enacted by the several States, each for itself, latterly by the legislature of the new German Empire. Finally, after twenty-two years of labour, a new Code for the whole German Empire was settled, was passed by the Chambers, and came into force on the first of January, 1900. It does not, however, altogether supersede pre-existing local law. This Code, far from being pure Roman law, embodies many rules due to mediaeval custom (especially custom relating to land-rights) modernized to suit modern conditions, and also a great deal of post-mediaeval legislation[2]. Some German jurists complain that it is too Teutonic; others that it is not Teutonic enough. One may perhaps conclude from these opposite criticisms that the codifiers have made a judiciously impartial use of both Germanic and Roman materials.

Speaking broadly, it may be said that the groundwork of both the French and the German Codes—that is to say their main lines and their fundamental legal conceptions—is Roman. Just as the character and genius of a language are determined by its grammar, irrespective

[1] Among the States in which the French Code has been taken as a model are Belgium, Italy, Spain, Portugal, Mexico, and Chile. See an article by Mr. E. Schuster in the *Law Quarterly Review* for January, 1896.

[2] An interesting sketch of the 'reception' of Roman law in Germany (by Dr. Erwin Grüber) may be found in the Introduction to Mr. Ledlie's translation of Sohm's *Institutionen* (1st edition).

of the number of foreign words it may have picked up, so Roman law remains Roman despite the accretion of the new elements which the needs of modern civilization have required it to accept.

The fifth stage is the transplantation of Roman law in its modern forms to new countries. The Spaniards and Portuguese, the French, the Dutch, and the Germans have carried their respective systems of law with them into the territories they have conquered and the colonies they have founded; and the law has often remained unchanged even when the territory or the colony has passed to new rulers. For law is a tenacious plant, even harder to extirpate than is language; and new rulers have generally had the sense to perceive that they had less to gain by substituting their own law for that which they found than they had to lose by irritating their new subjects. Thus, Roman-French law survives in Quebec (except in commercial matters) and in Louisiana, Roman-Dutch law in British Guiana, Ceylon and South Africa.

The cases of Poland, Russia and the Scandinavian kingdoms are due to a process different from any of those hitherto described. The law of Russia was originally Slavonic custom, influenced to some extent by the law of the Eastern Roman Empire, whence Russia took her Christianity and her earliest literary impulse. In its present shape, while retaining in many points a genuinely Slavonic character, and of course less distinctly Roman than is the law of France, it has drawn so much, especially as regards the principles of property rights and contracts, from the Code Napoléon and to a less degree from Germany, that it may be described as being Roman 'at the second remove,' and reckoned as an outlying and half-assimilated province, so to speak, of the legal realm of Rome. Poland, lying nearer Germany, and being, as a Roman Catholic country, influenced by the Canon Law, as well as by German teaching and German books, adopted rather more of Roman doctrine than Russia did[1]. Her students learnt Roman law first at Italian, afterwards at German Universities, and when they became judges, naturally applied its principles. The Scandinavian countries set out with a law purely Teutonic, and it is chiefly through the German Universities and the influence of German juridical literature that Roman principles have found their way in and coloured the old customs. Servia, Bulgaria and Rumania, on the other hand, were influenced during the Middle Ages by the law of the Eastern Empire, whence they drew their religion and their culture. Thus their modern law, whose character is due partly to these Byzantine influences—of course largely affected by Slavonic custom—and partly to what they have learnt from France and Austria, may also be referred to the Roman type.

The same may now be said of Japanese law. Among the changes which the people of the island empire of the Far East have made since their ancient feudal polity was overthrown in 1869, they have substituted for the mass of old customs varying from district to district, and enforced by the local magnates, a Code or body of regular modern law, based on that of modern European countries and especially on the German Code of A. D. 1900. Thus Japan also may be deemed to have claimed a share in the inheritance of the Roman law.

V. The Diffusion of English Law.

England, like Rome, has spread her law over a large part of the globe. But the process has been in her case not only far shorter but far simpler. The work has been (except as respects Ireland) effected within

[1] In Lithuania the rule was that where no express provision could be found governing a case, recourse should be had to 'the Christian laws.' Speaking generally, one may say that it was by and with Christianity that Roman law made its way in the countries to the east of Germany and to the north of the Eastern Empire.

the last three centuries; and it has been effected (except as regards Ireland and India) not by conquest but rather by peaceful settlement. This is one of the two points in which England stands contrasted with Rome. The other is that her own law has not been affected by the process. It has, within the seven centuries that lie between King Henry the Second and the present day, changed almost if not quite as much as the law of Rome changed in the seven centuries between the enactment of the Twelve Tables and the reign of Caracalla. But these changes have not been due, as those I have described in the Roman Empire were largely due, to the extension of the law of England to new subjects. They would apparently have come to pass in the same way and to the same extent had the English race remained confined to its own island.

England has extended her law over two classes of territories.

The first includes those which have been peacefully settled by men from the British Isles—North America (except Lower Canada), Newfoundland, Australia, New Zealand, Fiji and certain other isles in the Pacific Ocean, the Falkland Isles in the South Atlantic Ocean. All of these, except the United States, have remained politically connected with the British Crown.

The second includes conquered territories. In some of these, such as Wales, Ireland, Gibraltar, those parts of Canada which were ceded by France (except Quebec, to which we shall come presently), the pre-existing law has remained. In some few of the West India Islands, English law has been established as the only system, applicable to all subjects [1]. In others, such as Malta,

[1] It has undergone little or no change in the process. The Celtic customs disappeared in Wales; the Brehon law, though it was contained in many written texts and was followed over the larger part of Ireland till the days of the Tudors, has left practically no trace in the existing law of Ireland, which is, except as respects land, some penal matters, and marriage, virtually identical with the law of England.

Cyprus, Singapore, and India, English law is applied to Englishmen and native law to natives, the two systems being worked concurrently. Among these cases, that which presents problems of most interest and difficulty is India. But before we consider India, a few words may be given to the territories of the former class. They are now all of them, except the West Indies, the Pacific isles and the Falkland Isles, self-governing, and therefore capable of altering their own law. This they do pretty freely. The United States have now fifty-one legislatures at work, viz. Congress, forty-eight States, and two Organized Territories. They have turned out an immense mass of law since their separation from England. But immense as it is, and bold as are some of the experiments which may be found in it, the law of the United States remains (except of course in Louisiana) substantially English law. An English barrister would find himself quite at home in any Federal or State Court, and would have nothing new to master, except a few technicalities of procedure and the provisions of any statutes which might affect the points he had to argue. And the late patriarch of American teachers of law (Professor C. C. Langdell of the Law School in Harvard University), consistently declining to encumber his expositions with references to Federal or State Statutes, continued all his life to discourse on the Common Law of America, which differs little from the Common Law of England. The old Common Law which the settlers carried with them in the seventeenth century has of course been developed or altered by the decisions of American Courts. These, however, have not affected its thoroughly English character. Indeed, the differences between the doctrines enounced by the Courts of different States are sometimes just as great as the differences between the views of the Courts of Massachusetts or New Jersey and those of Courts in England.

The same is true of the self-governing British colonies. In them also legislation has introduced deviations from the law of the mother country. More than fifty years ago New Zealand, for instance, repealed the Statute of Uses, which is the corner-stone of English conveyancing; and the Australian legislatures have altered (among other things) the English marriage law. But even if the changes made by statute had been far greater than they have been, and even if there were not, as there still is, a right of appeal from the highest Courts of these colonies to the British Crown in Council, their law would still remain, in all its essential features, a genuine and equally legitimate offspring of the ancient Common Law.

We come now to the territories conquered by England, and to which she has given her law whether in whole or in part. Among these it is only of India that I shall speak, as India presents the phenomena of contact between the law of the conqueror and that of the conquered on the largest scale and in the most instructive form. What the English have done in India is being done or will have to be done, though nowhere else on so vast a scale, by the other great nations which have undertaken the task of ruling and of bestowing what they call the blessings of civilization upon the backward races. Russia, France, Germany, and now the United States also, all see this task before them. To them therefore, as well as to England, the experience of the British Government in India may be profitable.

VI. English Law in India.

When the English began to conquer India they found two great systems of customary law in existence there, the Musulman and the Hindu. There were other minor bodies of custom, prevailing among particular sects, but these may for the present be disregarded. The law of

Islam regulated the life and relations of all Musulmans; and parts of it, especially its penal provisions, were also applied by the Musulman potentates to their subjects generally, Hindus included. The Musulman law had been most fully worked out in the departments of family relations and inheritance, in some few branches of the law of contract, such as money loans and mortgages and matters relating to sale, and in the doctrine of charitable or pious foundations called Wakuf.

In the Hindu principalities, Hindu law was dominant, and even where the sovereign was a Musulman, the Hindu law of family relations and of inheritance was recognized as that by which Hindus lived. There were also of course many land customs, varying from district to district, which both Hindus and Musulmans observed, as they were not in general directly connected with religion. In some regions, such as what are now the United provinces of Oudh and Agra, these customs had been much affected by the land revenue system of the Mogul Emperors. It need hardly be said that where Courts of law existed, they administered an exceedingly rough and ready kind of justice, or perhaps injustice, for bribery and favouritism were everywhere rampant.

There were also mercantile customs, which were generally understood and observed by traders, and which, with certain specially Musulman rules recognized in Musulman States, made up what there was of a law of contracts.

Thus one may say that the law (other than purely religious law) which the English administrators in the days of Clive and Warren Hastings found consisted of—

First, a large and elaborate system of Inheritance and Family Law, the Musulman pretty uniform throughout India, though in some regions modified by Hindu custom, the Hindu less uniform. Each was utterly unlike English law and incapable of being fused with it. Each was closely bound up with the religion and social habits of the people. Each was contained in treatises of more or less antiquity and authority, some of the Hindu treatises very ancient and credited with almost divine sanction, the Musulman treatises of course posterior to the Koran, and consisting of commentaries upon that Book and upon the traditions that had grown up round it.

Secondly, a large mass of customs relating to the occupation and use of land and of various rights connected with tillage and pasturage, including water-rights, rights of soil-accretion on the banks of rivers, and forest-rights. The agricultural system and the revenue system of the country rested upon these land customs, which were of course mostly unwritten and which varied widely in different districts.

Thirdly, a body of customs, according to our ideas comparatively scanty and undeveloped, but still important, relating to the transfer and pledging of property, and to contracts, especially commercial contracts.

Fourthly, certain penal rules drawn from Musulman law and more or less enforced by Musulman princes.

Thus there were considerable branches of law practically non-existent. There was hardly any law of civil and criminal procedure, because the methods of justice were primitive, and would have been cheap, but for the prevalence of corruption among judges as well as witnesses. There was very little of the law of Torts or Civil Wrongs; and in the law of property, of contracts, and of crimes, some departments were wanting or in a rudimentary condition. Of a law relating to public and constitutional rights there could of course be no question, since no such rights existed.

In this state of facts the British officials took the line which practical men, having their hands full of other work, would naturally take, viz. the line of least resistance. They accepted and carried on what they found. Where there was a native law, they applied it, Musulman law to Musulmans, Hindu law to Hindus, and in the few places where they were to be found, Parsi law to Parsis, Jain law to Jains. Thus men of every creed —for it was creed, not race nor allegiance by which men were divided and classified in India—lived each according to his own law, as Burgundians and Franks and Romanized Gauls had done in the sixth century in Western Europe. The social fabric was not disturbed, for the land customs and the rules of inheritance were respected, and of course the minor officers, with whom chiefly the peasantry came in contact, continued to be natives. Thus the villager scarcely felt that he was passing under the dominion of an alien power, professing an alien faith. His life flowed on in the same equable course beside the little white mosque, or at the edge of the sacred grove. A transfer of power from a Hindu to a Musulman sovereign would have made more difference to him than did the establishment of British rule; and life was more placid than it would have been under either a rajah or a sultan, for the marauding bands which had been the peasants' terror were soon checked by European officers.

So things remained for more than a generation. So indeed things remain still as respects those parts of law which are inwoven with religion, viz. marriage, adoption (among Hindus) and other family relations, and also the succession to property. In all these matters native law continues to be administered by the Courts the English have set up; and when cases are appealed from the highest of those Courts to the Privy Council in England, that respectable body determines the true construction to be put on the Koran and the Islamic Traditions, or on passages from the mythical Manu, in the same business-like way as it would the meaning of an Australian statute[1]. Except in some few points to be presently noted, the Sacred Law of Islam and that of Brahmanism remain unpolluted by European ideas. Yet they have not stood unchanged, for the effect of the more careful and thorough examination which the contents of these two systems have received from advocates, judges, and text-writers, both native and English, imbued with the scientific spirit of Europe, has been to clarify and define them, and to develop out of the half-fluid material more positive and rigid doctrines than had been known before. Something like this may probably have been done by the Romans for the local or tribal law of their provinces.

In those departments in which the pre-existing customs were not sufficient to constitute a body of law large enough and precise enough for a civilized Court to work upon, the English found themselves obliged to supply the void. This was done in two ways. Sometimes the Courts boldly applied English law, being that which they knew. Sometimes they supplemented native custom by common sense, *i. e.* by their own ideas of what was just and fair. The phrase 'equity and good conscience' was used to embody the principles by which judges were to be guided when positive rules, statutory or customary, were not forthcoming. To a magistrate who knew no law at all, these words would mean that he might follow his own notions of 'natural justice,' and he would probably give more satisfaction to suitors than would his slightly more learned brother, trying to apply confused recollections of Blackstone or Chitty. In commercial matters common sense

[1] It is related that a hill tribe of Kols, in Central India, had a dispute with the Government of India over some question of forest-rights. The case having gone in favour of the Kols, the Government appealed to the Judicial Committee of the Privy Council. Shortly afterwards a passing traveller found the elders of the tribe assembled at the sacrifice of a kid. He inquired what deity was being propitiated, and was told that it was a deity powerful though remote, whose name was Privy Council.

would be aided by the usage of traders. In cases of Tort native custom was not often available, but as the magistrate who dealt out substantial justice would give what the people had rarely obtained from the native courts, they had no reason to complain of the change. As to rules of evidence, the young Anglo-Indian civilian would, if he were wise, forget all the English technicalities he might have learnt, and make the best use he could of his mother-wit [1].

For the first sixty years or more of British rule there was accordingly little or no attempt to Anglify the law of India, or indeed to give it any regular and systematic form. Such alterations as it underwent were the natural result of its being dispensed by Europeans. But to this general rule there were two exceptions, the law of Procedure and the law of Crimes. Courts had been established in the Presidency towns even before the era of conquest began. As their business increased and subordinate Courts were placed in the chief towns of the annexed provinces, the need for some regular procedure was felt. An Act of the British Parliament of A. D. 1781 empowered the Indian Government to make regulations for the conduct of the provincial Courts, as the Court at Fort William (Calcutta) had already been authorized to do for itself by an Act of 1773. Thus a regular system of procedure, modelled after that of England, was established; and the Act of 1781 provided that the rules and forms for the execution of process were to be accommodated to the religion and manners of the natives.

As respects penal law, the English began by adopting that which the Musulman potentates had been accustomed to apply. But they soon found that many of its provisions were such as a civilized and nominally Christian government could not enforce. Mutilation as

[1] For the facts given in the following pages I am much indebted to the singularly lucid and useful treatise of Sir C. P. Ilbert (formerly Legal Member of the Viceroy's Council) entitled *The Government of India.*

a punishment for theft, for instance, and stoning for sexual offences, were penalties not suited to European notions; and still less could the principle be admitted that the evidence of a non-Musulman is not receivable against one of the Faithful. Accordingly a great variety of regulations were passed amending the Musulman law of crimes from an English point of view. In Calcutta the Supreme Court did not hesitate to apply English penal law to natives; and applied it to some purpose at a famous crisis in the fortunes of Warren Hastings when (in 1775) it hanged Nuncomar for forgery under an English statute of 1728, which in the opinion of many high authorities of a later time had never come into force at all in India. It was inevitable that the English should take criminal jurisdiction into their own hands—the Romans had done the same in their provinces—and inevitable also that they should alter the penal law in conformity with their own ideas. But they did so in a very haphazard fashion. The criminal law became a patchwork of enactments so confused that it was the first subject which invited codification in that second epoch of English rule which we are now approaching.

Before entering on this remarkable epoch, one must remember that the English in India, still a very small though important class, were governed entirely by English law. So far as common law and equity went, this law was exactly the same as the contemporaneous law of England. But it was complicated by the fact that a number of Regulations, as they were called, had been enacted for India by the local government, that many British statutes were not intended to apply and probably did not apply to India (though whether they did or not was sometimes doubtful), and that a certain number of statutes had been enacted by Parliament expressly for India. Thus though the law under which the English lived had not been perceptibly affected by Indian customs, it was very confused and troublesome to work. That the learning of the judges sent from home to sit in the Indian Courts was seldom equal to that of the judges in England was not necessarily a disadvantage, for in traversing the jungle of Indian law the burden of English case lore would have too much impeded the march of justice.

The first period of English rule, the period of rapid territorial extension and of improvised government, may be said to have ended with the third Maratha war of 1817-8. The rule of Lord Amherst and Lord William Bentinck (1823-35) was a comparatively tranquil period, when internal reforms had their chance, as they had in the Roman Empire under Hadrian and Antoninus Pius. This was also the period when a spirit of legal reform was on foot in England. It was the time when the ideas of Bentham had begun to bear fruit, and when the work begun by Romilly was being carried on by Brougham and others. Both the law applied to Englishmen, and such parts of native law as had been cut across, filled up, and half re-shaped by English legal notions and rules, called loudly for simplification and reconstruction.

The era of reconstruction opened with the enactment in the India Charter Act of 1833, of a clause declaring that a general judicial system and a general body of law ought to be established in India applicable to all classes, Europeans as well as natives, and that all laws and customs having legal force ought to be ascertained, consolidated, and amended. The Act then went on to provide for the appointment of a body of experts to be called the Indian Law Commission, which was to inquire into and report upon the Courts, the procedure and the law then existing in India. Of this commission Macaulay, appointed in 1833 legal member of the Governor-General's Council, was the moving spirit: and with it the work of codification began. It prepared a

Penal Code, which however was not passed into law until 1860, for its activity declined after Macaulay's return to England and strong opposition was offered to his draft by many of the Indian judges. A second Commission was appointed under an Act of 1853, and sat in England. It secured the enactment of the Penal Code, and of Codes of Civil and of Criminal Procedure. A third Commission was created in 1861, and drafted other measures. The Government of India demurred to some of the proposed changes and evidently thought that legislation was being pressed on rather too fast. The Commission, displeased at this resistance, resigned in 1870; and since then the work of preparing as well as of carrying through codifying Acts has mostly been done in India. The net result of the seventy-nine years that have passed since Macaulay set to work in 1834 is that Acts codifying and amending the law, and declaring it applicable to both Europeans and natives, have been passed on the topics following:—

Crimes (1860).

Criminal Procedure (1861, 1882, and 1898; republished with amendments in 1904).

Civil Procedure (1859 and 1882; superseded by the now existing Civil Procedure Code of 1908).

Evidence (1872).

Limitation of Actions (1877).

Specific Relief (1877).

Probate and Administration (1881).

Contracts (1872) (but only the general rules of contract with a few rules on particular parts of the subject).

Negotiable Instruments (1881) (but subject to native customs).

Besides these, codifying statutes have been passed which do not apply (at present) to all India, but only to parts of it, or to specified classes of the population, on the topics following:—

Trusts (1882).
Transfer of Property (1882).
Succession (1865).
Easements (1882).
Guardians and Wards (1890).

These statutes cover a large part of the whole field of law, so that the only important departments not yet dealt with are those of Torts or Civil Wrongs (on which a measure not yet enacted was prepared some years ago); certain branches of contract law, which it is not urgent to systematize because they give rise to lawsuits only in the large cities, where the Courts are quite able to dispose of them in a satisfactory way; Family Law, which it would be unsafe to meddle with, because the domestic customs of Hindus, Musulmans, and Europeans are entirely different; and Inheritance, the greater part of which is, for the same reason, better left to native custom. Some points have, however, been covered by the Succession Act already mentioned. Thus the Government of India appear to think that they have for the present gone as far as they prudently can in the way of enacting uniform general laws for all classes of persons. Further action might displease either the Hindus or the Musulmans, possibly both: and though there would be advantages in bringing the law of both these sections of the population into a more clear and harmonious shape, it would in any case be impossible to frame rules which would suit both of them, and would also suit the Europeans. Here Religion steps in, a force more formidable in rousing opposition or disaffection than any which the Romans had to fear.

In such parts of the law as are not covered by these enumerated Acts, Englishmen, Hindus and Musulmans continue to live under their respective laws. So do Parsis, Sikhs, Buddhists (most numerous in Burma), and Jains, save that where there is really no native law or custom that can be shown to exist, the judge will naturally apply the principles of English law, handling them, if he knows how, in an untechnical way. Thus beside the new stream of united law which has its source in the codifying Acts, the various older streams of law, each representing a religion, flow peacefully on.

The question which follows—What has been the action on the other of each of these elements? resolves itself into three questions:—

How far has English Law affected the Native Law which remains in force?

How far has Native Law affected the English Law which is in force?

How have the codifying Acts been framed—*i. e.* are they a compromise between the English and the native element, or has either predominated and given its colour to the whole mass?

The answer to the first question is that English influence has told but slightly upon those branches of native law which had been tolerably complete before the British conquest, and which are so interwoven with religion that one may almost call them parts of religion. The Hindu and Musulman customs which regulate the family relations and rights of succession have been precisely defined, especially those of the Hindus, which were more fluid than the Muslim customs, and were much less uniform over the whole country. Trusts have been formally legalized, and their obligation rendered stronger. Adoption has been regularized and stiffened, for its effects had been uncertain in their legal operation. Where several doctrines contended, one doctrine has been affirmed by the English Courts, especially by the Privy Council as ultimate Court of Appeal, and the others set aside. Moreover the Hindu law of Wills has been in some points supplemented by English legislation, and certain customs repugnant to European ideas, such as the self-immolation of the widow on the husband's funeral pyre, have been abolished. And in those parts of law which, though regulated by local custom, were not religious, some improvements have been effected. The rights of the agricultural tenant have been placed on a more secure basis. Forest-rights have been ascertained and defined, partly no doubt for the sake of the pecuniary interests which the Government claims in them, and which the peasantry do not always admit. But no attempt has been made to Anglify these branches of law as a whole.

On the other hand, the law applicable to Europeans only has been scarcely (if at all) affected by native law. It remains exactly what it is in England, except in so far as the circumstances of India have called for special statutes.

The third question is as to the contents of those parts of the law which are common to Europeans and Natives, that is to say, the parts dealt with by the codifying Acts already enumerated. Here English law has decisively prevailed. It has prevailed not only because it would be impossible to subject Europeans to rules emanating from a different and a lower civilization, but also because native custom did not supply the requisite materials. Englishmen had nothing to learn from natives as respects procedure or evidence. The native mercantile customs did not constitute a system even of the general principles of contract, much less had those principles been worked out in their details. Accordingly the Contract Code is substantially English, and where it differs from the result of English cases, the differences are due, not to the influence of native ideas or native usage, but to the views of those who prepared the Code, and who, thinking the English case-law susceptible of improvement, diverged from it here and there just as they might have diverged had they been preparing a Code to be enacted for England. There are, however, some points in which the Penal Code shows itself to be a system intended for India. The right of self-defence is expressed in wider terms than would be used in England, for Macaulay conceived that the slackness of the native in protecting himself by force made it desirable to depart a little in this respect from the English rules. Offences such as dacoity (brigandage by robber bands), attempts to bribe judges or witnesses, the use of torture by policemen, kidnapping, the offering of insult or injury to sacred places, have been dealt with more fully and specifically than would be necessary in a Criminal Code for England. Adultery has, conformably to the ideas of the East, been made a subject for criminal proceedings. Nevertheless these, and other similar deviations from English rules which may be found in the Codes enacted for Europeans and natives alike, do not affect the general proposition that the codes are substantially English. The conquerors have given their law to the conquered. When the conquered had a law of their own which this legislation has effaced, the law of the conquerors was better. Where they had one too imperfect to suffice for a growing civilization, the law of the conquerors was inevitable.

VII. The Working of the Indian Codes.

Another question needs to be answered. It has a twofold interest, because the answer not only affects the judgment to be passed on the course which the English Government in India has followed, but also conveys either warning or encouragement to England herself. This question is—How have these Indian Codes worked in practice? Have they improved the administration of justice? Have they given satisfaction to the people? Have they made it easier to know the law, to apply the law, to amend the law where it proves faulty?

When I travelled in India in 1888-9 I obtained opinions on these points from many persons competent to speak. There was a good deal of difference of view, but the general result seemed to be as follows. I take the four most important codifying Acts, as to which it was most easy to obtain profitable criticisms.

The two Procedure Codes, Civil and Criminal, were very generally approved. They were not originally creative work, but were produced by consolidating and simplifying a mass of existing statutes and regulations, which had become unwieldy and confused. Order was evoked out of chaos, a result which, though beneficial everywhere, was especially useful in the minor Courts, whose judges had less learning and experience than those of the five High Courts at Calcutta, Madras, Bombay, Allahabad and Lahore.

The Penal Code was universally approved; and it deserves the praise bestowed on it, for it is one of the noblest monuments of Macaulay's genius. To appreciate its merits, one must remember how much, when prepared in 1834, it stood above the level of the English criminal law of that time. The subject is eminently fit to be stated in a series of positive propositions, and so far as India was concerned, it had rested mainly upon statutes and not upon common law. It has been dealt with in a scientific, but also in a practical common-sense way: and the result is a body of rules which are comprehensible and concise. To have these on their desks has been an immense advantage for magistrates in the country districts, many of whom have had but a scanty legal training. It has also been claimed for this Code that under it crime has enormously diminished: but how much of the diminution is due to the application of a clear and just system of rules, how much to the more efficient police administration, is a question on which I cannot venture to pronounce [1].

[1] The merits of this Code are discussed in an interesting and suggestive manner by Mr. H. Speyer in an article entitled *Le Droit Pénal Anglo-indien*, which appeared in the *Revue de l'Université de Bruxelles* in April, 1900.

No similar commendation was bestowed on the Evidence Code. Much of it was condemned as being too metaphysical, yet deficient in subtlety. Much was deemed superfluous, and because superfluous, possibly perplexing. Yet even those who criticized its drafting admitted that it might possibly be serviceable to untrained magistrates and practitioners, and I have myself heard some of these untrained men declare that they did find it helpful. They are a class relatively larger in India than in England.

It was with regard to the merits of the Contract Code that the widest difference of opinion existed. Any one who reads it can see that its workmanship is defective. It is neither exact nor subtle, and its language is often far from lucid. Every one agreed that Sir J. F. Stephen (afterwards Mr. Justice Stephen), who put it into the shape in which it was passed during his term of office as Legal Member of Council, and was also the author of the Evidence Act, was a man of great industry, much intellectual force, and warm zeal for codification. But his capacity for the work of drafting was deemed not equal to his fondness for it. He did not shine either in fineness of discrimination or in delicacy of expression. Indian critics, besides noting these facts, went on to observe that in country places four-fifths of the provisions of the Contract Act were superfluous, while those which were operative sometimes unduly fettered the discretion of the magistrate or judge, entangling him in technicalities, and preventing him from meting out that substantial justice which is what the rural suitor needs. The judge cannot disregard the Act, because if the case is appealed, the Court above, which has only the notes of the evidence before it, and does not hear the witnesses, is bound to enforce the provisions of the statute. In a country like India, law ought not to be too rigid: nor ought rights to be stiffened up so strictly as they are by this Contract Act.

Creditors had already, through the iron regularity with which the British Courts enforce judgments by execution, obtained far more power over debtors than they possessed in the old days, and more than the benevolence of the English administrator approves. The Contract Act increases this power still further. This particular criticism does not reflect upon the technical merits of the Act in itself. But it does suggest reasons which would not occur to a European mind, why it may be inexpedient by making the law too precise to narrow the path in which the judge has to walk. A strict administration of the letter of the law is in semi-civilized communities no unmixed blessing.

So much for the rural districts. In the Presidency cities, on the other hand, the Contract Code is by most experts pronounced to be unnecessary. The judges and the bar are already familiar with the points which it covers, and find themselves—so at least many of them say—rather embarrassed than aided by it. They think it cramps their freedom of handling a point in argument. They prefer the elasticity of the common law. And in point of fact, they seem to make no great use of the Act, but to go on just as their predecessors did before it was passed.

These criticisms may need to be discounted a little, in view of the profound conservatism of the legal profession, and of the dislike of men trained at the Temple or Lincoln's Inn to have anything laid down or applied on the Hooghly which is not being done at the same moment on the Thames. And a counterpoise to them may be found in the educational value which is attributed to the Code by magistrates and lawyers who have not acquired a mastery of contract law through systematic instruction or through experience at home. To them the Contract Act is a manual comparatively short and simple, and also authoritative; and they find it useful in enabling them to learn their business. On the whole, therefore, though the Code does not deserve the credit which has sometimes been claimed for it, one may hesitate to pronounce its enactment a misfortune. It at any rate provides a basis on which a really good Code of contractual law may some day be erected.

Taking the work of Indian codification as a whole, it has certainly benefited the country. The Penal Code and the two Codes of Procedure represent an unmixed gain. The same may be said of the consolidation of the statute law, for which so much was done by the energy and skill of Mr. Whitley Stokes. And the other codifying acts have on the whole tended both to improve the substance of the law and to make it more accessible. Their operation has, however, been less complete than most people in Europe realize, for while many of them are confined to certain districts, others are largely modified by the local customs which they have (as expressed in their saving clauses) very properly respected. If we knew more about the provinces of the Roman Empire we might find that much more of local custom subsisted side by side with the apparently universal and uniform imperial law than we should gather from reading the compilations of Justinian.

It has already been observed that Indian influences have scarcely at all affected English law as it continues to be administered to Englishmen in India. Still less have they affected the law of England at home. It seems to have been fancied thirty or forty years ago, when law reform in general and codification in particular occupied the public mind more than they do now, that the enactment of codes of law for India, and the success which was sure to attend them there, must react upon England and strengthen the demand for the reduction of her law into a concise and systematic form. No such result has followed. The desire for codification in England has not been perceptibly strengthened by the experience of India. Nor can it indeed be said that the experience of India has taught jurists or statesmen much which they did not know before. That a good code is a very good thing, and that a bad code is, in a country which possesses competent judges, worse than no code at all—these are propositions which needed no Indian experience to verify them. The imperfect success of the Evidence and Contract Acts has done little more than add another illustration to those furnished by the Civil Code of California and the Code of Procedure in New York of the difficulty which attends these undertakings. Long before Indian codification was talked of, Savigny had shown how hard it is to express the law in a set of definite propositions without reducing its elasticity and impeding its further development. His arguments scarcely touch penal law, still less the law of procedure, for these are not topics in which much development need be looked for. But the future career of the Contract Act and of the projected Code of Torts, when it comes to be enacted, may supply some useful data for testing the soundness of his doctrine.

One reason why these Indian experiments have so little affected English opinion may be found in the fact that few Englishmen have either known or cared anything about them. The British public has not realized how small is the number of persons by whom questions of legal policy in India have during the last eighty years been determined. Two or three officials in Downing Street and as many in Calcutta have practically controlled the course of events, with little interposition from outside. Even when Commissions have been sitting, the total number of those whose hand is felt has never exceeded a dozen. It was doubtless much the same in the Roman Empire. Indeed the world seldom realizes by how few persons it is governed. There is a sense in which power may be said to rest with the whole community, and there is also a sense in which it may be said, in some governments, to rest with a single autocrat. But in reality it almost always rests in every country with an extremely small number of persons, whose knowledge and will prevail over or among the titular possessors of authority.

Before we attempt to forecast the future of English law in India, let us cast a glance back at the general course of its history as compared with that of the law of Rome in the ancient world.

VIII. Comparison of the Roman Law with English Law in India

Rome grew till her law became first that of Italy, then that of civilized mankind. The City became the World, *Urbs* became *Orbis,* to adopt the word-play which was once so familiar. Her law was extended over her Empire by three methods:—

Citizenship was gradually extended over the provinces till at last all subjects had become citizens.

Many of the principles and rules of the law of the City were established and diffused in the provinces by the action of Roman Magistrates and Courts, and especially by the Provincial Edict.

The ancient law of the City was itself all the while amended, purged of its technicalities, and simplified in form, till it became fit to be the law of the World.

Thus, when the law of the City was formally extended to the whole Empire by the grant of citizenship to all subjects, there was not so much an imposition of the conqueror's law upon the conquered as the completion of a process of fusion which had been going on for fully four centuries. The fusion was therefore natural; and because it was natural it was complete and final. The separation of the one great current of Roman law into various channels, which began in the fifth century A. D. and has continued ever since, has been due to purely historical causes, and of late years (as we shall see presently) the streams that flow in these channels have tended to come nearer to one another.

During the period of more than four centuries (B. C. 241 to A. D. 211-7), when these three methods of development and assimilation were in progress, the original law of the City was being remoulded and amended in the midst of and under the influence of a non-Roman population of aliens (*peregrini*) at Rome and in the provinces, and that semi-Roman law which was administered in the provinces was being created by magistrates and judges who lived in the provinces and who were, after the time of Tiberius, mostly themselves of provincial origin. Thus the intelligence, reflection, and experience of the whole community played upon and contributed to the development of the law. Judges, advocates, juridical writers and teachers as well as legislators, joined in the work. The completed law was the outcome of a truly national effort. Indeed it was largely through making a law which should be fit for both Italians and provincials that the Romans of the Empire became almost a nation.

In India the march of events has been different, because the conditions were different. India is ten thousand miles from England. The English residents are a mere handful.

The Indian races are in a different stage of civilization from the English. They are separated by religion; they are separated by colour.

There has therefore been no fusion of English and native law. Neither has there been any movement of the law of England to adapt itself to become the law of her Indian subjects. English law has not, like Roman, come halfway to meet the provinces. It is true that no such approximation was needed, because English law had already reached, a century ago, a point of development more advanced than Roman law had reached when the conquest of the provinces began, and the process of divesting English law of its archaic technicalities went on so rapidly during the nineteenth century under purely home influences, that neither the needs of India nor the influences of India came into the matter at all.

The Romans had less resistance to meet with from religious diversities than the English have had, for the laws of their subjects had not so wrapped their roots round religious belief or usage as has been the case in India. But they had more varieties of provincial custom to consider, and they had, especially in the laws of the Hellenized provinces, systems more civilized and advanced, first to recognize and ultimately to supersede, than any body of law which the English found.

There is no class in India fully corresponding to the Roman citizens domiciled in the provinces during the first two centuries of the Roman Empire. The European British subjects, including the Eurasians, are comparatively few, and they are to a considerable extent a transitory element, whose true home is England. Only to a very small extent do they enjoy personal immunities and privileges such as those that made Roman citizenship so highly prized, for the English, more liberal than the Romans, began by extending to all natives of India, as and when they became subjects of the British Crown, the ordinary rights of British subjects enjoyed under such statutes as Magna Charta and the Bill of Rights. The natives of India have entered into the labours of the barons at Runnymede and of the Whigs of 1688.

What has happened has been that the English have given to India such parts of their own law (somewhat simplified in form) as India seemed fitted to receive. These parts have been applied to Europeans as well as to natives, but they were virtually applicable to Europeans before codification began. The English rulers have filled up those departments in which there was no native law worthy of the name, sometimes, however, respecting local native customs. Here one finds an interesting parallel to the experience of the Romans. They, like the English, found criminal law and the law of procedure to be the departments which could be most easily and promptly dealt with. They, like the English, were obliged to acquiesce in the retention by a part of the population of some ancient customs regarding the Family and the Succession to Property. But this acquiescence was after all partial and local; whereas the English have neither applied to India the more technical parts of their own law, such as that relating to land, nor attempted to supersede those parts of native law which are influenced by religion, such as the parts which include family relations and inheritance. Thus there has been no general fusion comparable to that which the beginning of the third century A. D. saw in the Roman Empire.

As respects codification, the English have in one sense done more than the Romans, in another sense less. They have reduced such topics as penal law and procedure, evidence and trusts, to a compact and well-ordered shape, which is more than Justinian did for any part of the Roman law. But they have not brought the whole law together into one Corpus Iuris, and they have left large parts of it in triplicate, so to speak, that is to say, consisting of rules which are entirely different for Hindus, for Musulmans, and for Europeans.

Moreover, as it is the law of the conquerors which has in India been given to the conquered practically unaffected by native law, so also the law of England has not been altered by the process. It has not been substantially altered in India. The uncodified English law there is the same (local statutes excepted) as the law of England at home. Still less has it been altered in England itself. Had Rome not acquired her Empire, her law would never have grown to be what it was in Justinian's time. Had Englishmen never set foot in India, their law would have been, so far as we can tell, exactly what it is to-day.

Neither have those natives of India who correspond to the provincial subjects of Rome borne any recognizable share in the work of Indian legal development. Some of them have, as text-writers or as judges, rendered good service in elucidating the ancient Hindu customs. But the work of throwing English law into the codified form in which it is now applied in India to Europeans and natives alike has been done entirely by Englishmen. In this respect also the more advanced civilization has shown its dominant creative force.

IX. The Future of English Law in India.

Here, however, it is fit to remember that we are not, as in the case of the Romans, studying a process which has been completed. For them it was completed before the fifth century saw the dissolution of the western half of the Empire. For India it is still in progress. Little more than a century has elapsed since English rule was firmly established; only half a century since the Punjab and (shortly afterwards) Oudh were annexed. Although the Indian Government has prosecuted the work of codification much less actively during the last thirty years than in the twenty years preceding, and seems to conceive that as much has now been done as can safely be done at present, still in the long future that seems to lie before British rule in India the equalization and development of law may go much further than we can foresee to-day. The power of Britain is at this moment stable, and may remain so if she continues to hold the sea and does not provoke discontent by excessive taxation.

Two courses which legal development may follow are conceivable. One is that all those departments of law whose contents are not determined by conditions peculiar to India will be covered by further codifying acts, applicable to Europeans and natives alike, and that therewith the process of equalization and assimilation will stop because its natural limits will have been reached. The other is that the process will continue until the law of the stronger and more advanced race has absorbed that of the natives and become applicable to the whole Empire.

Which of these two things will happen depends upon the future of the native religions, and especially of Hinduism and of Islam, for it is in religion that the legal customs of the natives have their roots. Upon this vast and dark problem it may seem idle to speculate; nor can it be wholly dissevered from a consideration of the possible future of the religious beliefs which now hold sway among Europeans. Both Islam and Hinduism are professed by masses of human beings so huge, so tenacious of their traditions, so apparently inaccessible to European influences, that no considerable declension of either faith can be expected within a long period of years. Yet experience, so far as it is available, goes to show that no form of heathenism, not even an ancient and in some directions highly cultivated form like Hinduism, does ultimately withstand the solvent power of European science and thought. Even now, though Hinduism is growing every day among the hill-folk, at the expense of the ruder superstitions which have hitherto formed their religion, it is losing its hold on the educated class, and it sees every day members of its lower castes pass over to Islam, whereas none pass from Islam to it. So Islam also, deeply rooted as it may seem to be, wanes in the presence of Christianity, and though it advances in

Central Africa, declines in the Mediterranean countries. It has hitherto declined not by the conversion of its members to other faiths, but by the diminution of the Muslim population and through the recovery by Christian races of regions which Islam conquered in the days of its power; yet one must not assume that when the Turkish Sultanate or Khalifate has vanished, it may not lose much of its present hold upon the Nearer and even perhaps upon the Further East. Possibly both Hinduism and Islam may, so potent are the new forces of change now at work in India, begin within a century or two to show signs of approaching dissolution. Polygamy may by that time have disappeared. Other peculiar features of the law of family and inheritance will tend to follow, though some may survive through the attachment to habit even when their original religious basis has been forgotten.

In the Arctic seas, a ship sometimes lies for weeks together firmly bound in a vast ice-field. The sailor who day after day surveys from the masthead the dazzling expanse sees on every side nothing but a solid surface, motionless and apparently immovable. Yet all the while this ice-field is slowly drifting to the south, carrying with it the embedded ship. At last, when a warmer region has been reached and the south wind has begun to blow, that which overnight was a rigid and glittering plain is in the light of dawn a tossing mass of ice-blocks, each swiftly melting into the sea, through which the ship finds her homeward path. So may it be with these ancient religions. When their dissolution comes, it may come with unexpected suddenness, for the causes which will produce it will have been acting simultaneously and silently over a wide area. If the English are then still the lords of India, there will be nothing to prevent their law from becoming (with some local variations) the law of all India. Once established there is the same (local statutes excepted) as the law whatever political changes may befall, for nothing clings to the soil more closely than a body of civilized law once well planted. So the law of England may become the permanent heritage, not only of the hundreds of millions who will before the time we are imagining be living beyond the Atlantic, but of those hundreds of millions who fill the fertile land between the Straits of Manaar and the long rampart of Himalayan snows.

We embarked on this inquiry for the sake of ascertaining what light the experience of the English in India throws upon the general question of the relation of the European nations to those less advanced races over whom they are assuming dominion, and all of whom will before long own some controlling authority of European origin[1].

These races fall into two classes, those which do and those which do not possess a tolerably complete system of law. Turks, Persians, Egyptians, Moors, and perhaps Siamese belong to the former class; all other non-European races to the latter.

As to the latter there is no difficulty. So soon as Kafirs or Mongols or Hausas have advanced sufficiently to need a regular set of legal rules, they will (if their European masters think it worth while) become subject to the law of those masters, of course more or less differentiated according to local customs or local needs. It may be assumed that French law will prevail in Madagascar, and English law in Uganda, and Russian law in the regions along the Amur.

Where, however, as is the case in the Musulman and perhaps also in the Buddhist countries belonging to the former class, a legal system which, though imperfect,

[1] Among the 'less advanced races' one must of course not now include the Japanese, but one may include the Turks and the Persians. The fate of China still hangs in the balance. She is not at all likely to be ruled,—nor is it to be wished that she should be ruled,—though she must come to be influenced, and probably more and more influenced, by European ideas.

especially on the commercial side, has been carefully worked out in some directions, holds the field and rests upon religion, the question is less simple. The experience of the English in India suggests that European law will occupy the non-religious parts of the native systems, and will tend by degrees to encroach upon and permeate even the religious parts, though so long as Islam (or Brahmanism) maintains its sway the legal customs and rules embedded in religion will survive. No wise ruler would seek to efface them so far as they are neither cruel nor immoral. It is only these ancient religions—Hinduism, Buddhism, and especially Islam—that can or will resist, though perhaps only for a time, and certainly only partially, the rising tide of European law.

X. Present Position of Roman and English Law in the World.

European law means, as we have seen, either Roman law or English law, so the last question is: Will either, and if so which, of these great rival systems prevail over the other?

They are not unequally matched. The Roman jurists, if we include Russian as a sort of modified Roman law, influence at present a greater number of human beings, but Bracton and Coke and Mansfield might rejoice to perceive that the doctrines which they expounded are being diffused even more swiftly, with the swift diffusion of the English tongue, over the globe. It is an interesting question, this competitive advance of legal systems, and one which would have engaged the attention of historians and geographers, were not law a subject which lies so much outside the thoughts of the lay world that few care to study its historical bearings. It furnishes a remarkable instance of the tendency of strong types to supplant and extinguish weak ones in the domain of social development. The world is, or will shortly be, practically divided between two sets of legal conceptions of rules, and two only. The elder had its birth in a small Italian city, and though it has undergone endless changes and now appears in a variety of forms, it retains its distinctive character, and all these forms still show an underlying unity. The younger has sprung from the union of the rude customs of a group of Low German tribes with rules worked out by the subtle, acute and eminently disputatious intellect of the Gallicized Norsemen who came to England in the eleventh century. It has been much affected by the elder system, yet it has retained its distinctive features and spirit, a spirit specially contrasted with that of the imperial law in everything that pertains to the rights of the individual and the means of asserting them. And it has communicated something of this spirit to the more advanced forms of the Roman law in constitutional countries.

At this moment the law whose foundations were laid in the Roman Forum commands a wider area of the earth's surface, and determines the relations of a larger mass of mankind. But that which looks back to Westminster Hall sees its subjects increase more rapidly, through the growth of the United States and the British Colonies, and has a prospect of ultimately overspreading India also. Neither is likely to overpower or absorb the other. But it is possible that they may draw nearer, and that out of them there may be developed, in the course of ages, a system of rules of private law which shall be practically identical so far as regards contracts and property and civil wrongs, possibly as regards offences also. Already the commercial law of all civilized countries is in substance the same everywhere, that is to say, it guarantees rights and provides remedies which afford equivalent securities to men in their dealings with one another and bring them to the same goal by slightly different paths.

The more any department of law lies within the domain of economic interest, the more do the rules that belong to it tend to become the same in all countries, for in the domain of economic interest Reason and Science have full play. But the more the element of human emotion enters any department of law, as for instance that which deals with the relations of husband and wife, or of parent and child, or that which defines the freedom of the individual as against the State, the greater becomes the probability that existing divergences between the laws of different countries may in that department continue, or even that new divergences may appear.

Still, on the whole, the progress of the world is towards uniformity in law, and towards a more evident uniformity than is discoverable either in the sphere of religious beliefs or in that of political institutions.

INDEX